OUR SUSTAINABLE FUTURE

Series Editors

Charles A. Francis
University of Nebraska–Lincoln

Cornelia Flora
Iowa State University

Paul A. Olson
University of Nebraska–Lincoln

Green Plans

BLUEPRINT FOR A SUSTAINABLE EARTH

HUEY D. JOHNSON With a
new afterword by the author

University of Nebraska Press
Lincoln and London

Library of Congress
Cataloging-in-Publication Data
Johnson, Huey D.
Green plans : blueprint for a sustainable earth
/ Huey D. Johnson; with a new afterword by
the author. — 3rd ed.
p. cm. — (Our sustainable future)
Includes bibliographical references and index.
ISBN 978-0-8032-6020-7 (pbk. : alk. paper)
1. Environmental policy. 2. Sustainable
development. 3. Green movement. I. Title.
GE195.J64 2008
333.7—dc22   2007037354
Set in Sabon by Bob Reitz.
Designed by Ashley Muehlbauer.

Contents

Figures

Acknowledgments

In writing this third edition I've been blessed with the assistance of Bonnie Durrance. She is a skilled editor, writer, and photographer. And she is a caring environmental thinker who is making a difference in the world. Her ideas and suggestions were instrumental in the preparation of this book.

There are many others I would like to thank who generously contributed their time and thoughts to the contents of this book. Among them are Peggy Lauer, Mike Painter, Tyler Johnson, Phillip A. Greenberg, Erika Bley, Jake Kosek, A. Michael Signer, Ann Kelly, Craig Lawson, Eric Brandsma, Jessica Presson, and Jason Morrison. Their efforts and insights have been invaluable.

On chapter 5, "The Netherlands," I welcomed the assistance of Herman Sips, an expert on the Dutch Green Plan. He also had the knowledge I needed to confirm the information in the chapter on the European Union. Hans Van Ziest, a second Dutch expert on the National Environmental Policy Plan, also critiqued the chapter.

For chapter 6, "New Zealand," I had the help of Dr. Tom Fookes, one of the originators of the New Zealand Resource Management Act.

My thanks and appreciation also go to the Green Planners and other government officials and their staffs, the environmentalists, and the businesspeople of the Netherlands, New Zealand, Canada, the United States, and all the other nations mentioned here for taking the time from their busy lives to explain their countries' policies to me, and for having the vision and courage to carry out their nations' green plans.

Introduction

It has been twelve years since the first edition of this book. In it I described Green Planning as a concept of great importance and a promising step toward solving environmental problems. Since then, the environmental programs of most nations have not kept pace with the growth of those problems, which are now capped off by the arrival of the huge threat of global warming. Nonetheless, I'm pleased to say that in certain countries, principally the Netherlands, Singapore, and New Zealand, Green Planning has shown exemplary success as a way to work toward social, economic, and environmental sustainability.

These past eighteen years of successful environmental management offer many valuable lessons to other nations, states, cities, corporations, and institutions that need to get on with environmental quality management. The purpose of this third edition is to describe the ongoing idea and show how it is working. To this project I bring the benefit of my own forty years of experience as an environmentalist and planner, as well as the work of the Resource Renewal Institute (RRI), which I founded in 1983 to study and promote Green Plans.

When I first looked at Green Plans as environmental policy, I thought the Dutch example was outstanding. I still do. Their plan, known as the NEPP, the National Environmental Policy Plan, has been functioning now for eighteen years. That length of time is important because for any program to be able to change a society's environmental policies on a Green Plan scale, the policy needs to survive over time. The eighteen years of Holland's successful Green Plan is the driving reason for the third edition of this book.

Recently, as I was pondering the reasons for that success, I received a note from one of the Dutch pioneers in Green Planning, who summarized in a nutshell why Green Plans have worked so well in the Netherlands. Among his key points are: leadership, long-term goals, short-term targets, scale, a level playing field, the integration of environment, economy, and land zoning, and participatory process. I'll be exploring and commenting on these and other factors contributing to the success of Green Plans in the course of this book.

While the success of Green Plans has been impressive, especially in the case of the Netherlands, New Zealand, and Singapore, it has not been universal. Canada's Green Plan, for example, has evaporated. But valuable lessons can also be learned from examples of failure.

For me, the most difficult part of thinking about and writing this update is watching the lack of progress of the Green Plan idea in the United States. When a governor in one state launched it, his successor ignored it and let the beginning effort toward a Green Plan wilt. That doesn't mean that a great deal wasn't accomplished here and there, but we cannot today see anywhere in the United States a program of the needed scale, much less duration, required to solve our own environmental problems.

So, you might ask, why Green Plans? The examples of Holland and New Zealand and Singapore prove that in order to solve the environmental problem, you have to solve the *whole* problem, not selected parts. Green Plans approach the problem in a way in which we have never approached it before, this time in a serious effort to *solve* it. Green Plans are about believing that we can put the problem behind us, as we put polio behind us—and in the process, find that we all benefit when we work together.

Green Plans are about rescuing the concept of planning from the scrap heap of history. Planning seemed so good and so important back in the 1950s and 1960s, but then it simply became an excuse for not making a political decision, and the enthusiasm for it faded abruptly. The elected, decision-making body, to avert political pressure, would continue to request study after study until the project was deemed to be unworkable and the applicant would just "go away." I realize now that, in terms of the environment, the difficulty with planning was that we were not looking at the problem on a large enough scale. We did not have a structure that was comprehensive enough to do what had to be done—that is, to approach the problem with the intention of solving it.

After eighteen years, Green Plans show what planning can and should be. They are comprehensive, integrated, and large scale—three characteristics that are central to solving environmental problems, whether on the local, regional, or national level. I have studied endless alternatives and read what now seem to be thousands of proposals and philosophical discourses, all discussing topics related to this central dilemma of declining environmental quality. But in all those documents, I do not remember one, other than Green Plans, that looked at the issue in terms of its actual scale and complexity, taking into consideration the entire set of relationships between air, soil, water, plants, animals, and people.

The individual pieces that go into making up any country's Green Plan are not revolutionary; most are not even new. What is so radical about what Green Plan countries are doing is the scope of their vision, the fact that they have pulled together all the related pieces into one package.

The point is that by creating an integrated approach, these countries have solved virtually all their local environmental problems. Because Green Plans are comprehensive, no one popular issue, such as wilderness preservation, rainforests, or toxics, dominates the overall strategy. An advantage of large scale is that each issue is an important part of the whole, and each gains more authority *because* it is part of a larger plan.

All the different issues and their constituencies are forged into an apolitical coalition that has as its goal the resolution of all problems. As a result, more people can relate to the many interests, and the plan gains popular and political support.

People take hope from such a large-scale effort because they can see that their government is serious in its commitment. The threat is thus turned into an asset, bringing people together and helping them to put conflict behind them. People are willing to make small sacrifices when they can see how big the pay-off will be—a livable future for their grandchildren—and when they understand that their entire society is working toward the same end.

Green Plan nations have accepted that natural resources are a complex, interrelated system and that any real environmental plan must be comprehensive enough to embrace that complexity. They have made environmental recovery their top priority and have set into motion large-scale efforts guided by the government and involving all segments of society. Their businesses and industries are thriving as a result. Whole societies have been improved. Green Plans are based on the critically important premise that our social and economic well-being depends on a healthy environment, and that we must manage our natural and physical environment in a sustainable fashion if we want to continue to meet our own needs and to allow future generations to meet theirs.

Such a dream, of course, requires focused, disciplined hard work, including the political work of selling the idea and involving people as a force. Only the people can cause government to make environmental recovery its first priority. This shift in priorities is essential: environmental recovery is a matter of survival. We have the technical knowledge and the resources to accomplish it, but in order to do so we must make it a priority, as we have in the past for bombs and rockets and space vehicles.

In summary, I offer this book in praise of Green Plans, to show what they are, how they have succeeded, and to serve as a central source of information for politicians, planners, students, activists, and anyone else interested in solving the environmental problem.

GREEN PLANS

PART I

Defining the Problem and Its Solution

A Commitment to Change

The hour may be late, but there is nothing that says that it is too late. There is nothing in man's plight that his vision, if he cared to cultivate it, and his will, if he cared to exercise it, could not alleviate. The challenge is to see what could be done and then have the heart and resolution to attempt it. —*George Kennan*

Despite the perilous state of our planetary environment, from climate change to the energy crisis, comprehensive environmental planning—Green Planning—as practiced in certain forward-looking countries is today bringing efficiency, cost reduction, and overall effectiveness to a wide variety of organizations including businesses, universities, churches, and others. In the process, it is contributing to a healthier life, a more vital and diverse natural world, the preservation of the resource base of our global economy and future development, and ultimately to our collective security. The success of comprehensive environmental planning can already be seen in the examples of a number of countries, several of which I will be discussing in this book, whose progress represents a large-scale advance toward solving humanity's environmental problems. These examples demonstrate that by working together, with imagination and innovation, problems can be solved at affordable costs, for the benefit of everyone.

AWAKENING FROM THE INDUSTRIAL DREAM

In this postindustrial age, we have come to realize that the great dream of the industrial age, delivering comfort and quantity to everybody, at prices they can afford, has brought along with it unexpected problems: pollution, environmental decline, degradation of nature, loss of species, and health risk to ourselves.

In the past, when the problems caused by these activities became too extreme to ignore, as when the air became too dirty to breathe or the water too polluted to drink, or a river became so choked with toxins it actually caught fire, we attempted to clean up—discovering in the process that it is better and cheaper to prevent the problems in the first place. But often, we ignored warnings about pollution and overexploitation, and as a result, have pushed some resources beyond their capacity to recover. In some areas, where there were formerly productive resource-based industries, people can no longer find food or work.

Now, as industries have grown up and populations have increased and the needs of these new millions have spurred industries to even greater growth, the pressures on the environment have reached the tipping point. Problems are no longer local but regional and continental. The current attention to global warming is awakening us to the realization that what we do can affect the entire planet. We see images now that would have seemed impossible a short time ago. The polar ice caps are melting and the polar bears face extinction. The oceans themselves are dying. The Mediterranean fisheries, once so prolific, are depleted. The Pacific Coast fishery of North America, once home to a thriving sardine industry employing twenty-five thousand people in California alone, also has diminished. Now, we can look back to the novels of John Steinbeck to remind us of humanity's impact on a once-great resource.

We've arrived at this point because over the years people of influence and leaders of industry refused to acknowledge that environmental problems were real. Over the past fifty years, these leaders, who were and are the economic voices of the nation, fought tooth and nail against what they perceived as a threat to their dream, their own prosperity. Their driving motive is always the bottom line, the quarterly corporate report. These short-term corporate financial statements, whether they are meant to do so or not, run the economy. And that reality impacts the long-term health of the environment. Now, the bottom line is health and life itself.

Another part of the problem is that government leadership in the United States has not been active enough, nor has Congress given industry incentives to adopt a new management approach to prevent pollution from continuing to spill out into the landscape, poisoning streams, rivers, oceans, land, and air. When incentives were proposed they were usually argued against in court or government scientists would try to downplay the serious nature of the problems.

Some enlightened companies are working toward change, but others, fossil fuel industries, for example, are making a profit as things are now, and that's their interest, period. The old guard industrial leaders will say a free hand (deregulation) is necessary for healthy competition and prosperity. And while that may be true to a degree, experience is teaching us that such freedom has to include environmental management, otherwise, life as we know it is going to be lost. And that is unacceptable.

WHAT ARE WE TO DO ABOUT THESE PROBLEMS?

The Netherlands mobilized its environmental program in 1988, following a warning by Queen Beatrix in her annual Christmas speech. She told the Dutch people that the future of life itself could be at stake, leaving little doubt that their society, if it was to survive, had to change. Some members of industry, instead of resisting, as they had been, joined in to assume cooperative leadership. This in itself was a huge, powerful change. The companion marvels were the support of the labor movement, the involvement of the Dutch Parliament, and finally, the involvement of the nonprofit environmental community, which served a very important watchdog role. Even though the entire business community didn't jump on board immediately, enough did so that they were able to set a framework for change and establish programs that have become the foremost example of successful comprehensive environmental planning in the world.

IF THE DUTCH COULD DO IT,
WHY HASN'T THIS HAPPENED IN THE
UNITED STATES AND ELSEWHERE?

In the past we have always looked at one issue at a time, usually those advanced by a narrow special interest, passing air pollution legislation one year, devoting some funding to endangered species the next. But this piecemeal approach has not worked. The example of the Netherlands, and others, has shown us that a comprehensive approach works. They have shown that efficient management, focused on the shared goal of environmental health, can put our new organizational and technological knowledge to work in a way that leads to a healthy, sustainable society. This kind of management enables business not to be nailed to the letter of every page of detailed prescriptive legislation but, by establishing long-term targets and performance standards, to be able to set priorities and align necessary actions with the business cycle.

To advocate this new approach is not to belittle the extraordinarily valuable efforts made by so many people for so many years in fields as diverse as science, agriculture, technology, and finance. That we are now able to make a leap forward to put things into a better functioning whole is due in large part to their work. It is also due to the work of those who have sought to wake people up to the environmental crisis. Much of the world now accepts the seriousness of the problems we face, particularly with regard to global warming and air pollution, and is ready to undertake the major efforts necessary to halt and reverse the worldwide environmental damage.

However, even in Holland, over the years, environmental concerns have lost their ranking in the public eye. At this writing, the environment is about fourteenth on a list of fifteen priorities. People are on the one hand satisfied about progress, yet at the same time they say more stringent policies would be welcomed. Global warming and air pollution are their main concerns.

THE WHOLE IS GREATER THAN
THE SUM OF ITS PARTS

Because it is so new, the idea of solving the entire problem of environmental decline may sound impossible to many people: How can we solve the entire problem if we cannot even solve the smaller, individual issues? But that is precisely the power of a big-picture approach. By tackling the larger problem, you carry along a host of smaller ones. And by taking a longer time horizon, you have more flexibility and more time to set priorities that do not change from year to year, leaving problems unresolved. Rather, people get to decide within that larger time frame when changes best fit in.

I've observed this principle working in the political arena. For example, opposition to ideas within the legislative process traditionally focuses on the one theme the lobbyist or opposing advocate is paid to oppose. If that one item is expanded, say from a single water matter, such as the price of a cubic-foot-per-second flow, to a package of water related issues including the one the opponent is to oppose, they often will let the package go. I first observed this when an opponent of a water bill suddenly recognized that the broadened proposal included a provision that would improve fishing. He was a fisherman. Realizing the bill would help maintain a healthy fish stock, he switched his opposition to support for the package.

Comprehensive plans are the only way to solve large-scale problems. They reach beyond the individual issues to the problems created by the relationships *between* those issues. The reality of ecology is that we cannot solve the individual problems unless we include the relationships of each to the others. Within the comprehensive scale, even powerful, single-interest advocates such as my fisherman friend, can realize something positive. This is another reason why social, political, and economic factors need to be combined when planning improvement in environmental policy.

FLEXIBILITY IS THE KEY

In this comprehensive kind of thinking, one of the certainties is that some of the smaller parts will develop unpredictable problems. If all you're looking at is one part at a time, and that part develops a problem, you are likely to drill down into it and lose sight of the goal. So the importance of comprehensive thinking is that you keep a wide view and allow for the wandering possibilities of one or more of the problems within the whole to go awry and be corrected.

At the same time, individual successes lend strength to the whole. I've observed that when several individual concepts are banded together, they have tremendous power, much more than they would if standing alone. But to get there, people need to break out of certain narrow structures. This is difficult. It's almost a fact of human existence that whatever our experience is, that becomes our information base. So a corporate executive might go through a challenging training process but find that what he has learned can't be applied within the confines of the organization he works for. The changes he may want to make may seem costly or risky. If he tries, he may lose his job. If the company tries, at first, profits may go down. Still, paradoxically, change will be the key to their survival—and ours as well.

This way of looking at a spectrum of factors exposes a non-scientific reality. Though we would like to think that policy decisions should be based on hard science, it isn't always possible. There is always a collection of factors involved with decision making, particularly the involvement of the ever unpredictable factor of human personalities, which makes predicting any result a less than scientific exercise.

GREEN PLANS NEED INDUSTRY TO WORK

A tremendous gift of the Dutch industrial experience is its demonstrated success. The Dutch experience shows that industry is necessary to the success of environmental recovery. For any Green Plan to succeed, in any city, state, or nation, the corporate presence, as a source of so many environmental problems, and also a crucial element in the economy of a nation, is essential. But so far the chamber-of-commerce leadership followed by the majority of U.S. industry tends to resist anything that requires long-term thinking or change. This is understandable from a short-term point of view. If you're making a couple of million a year to keep the train you're running on the track you're on, you're not going to go risking that couple of million a year changing tracks. That is one reason the powerful fossil-fuel interests reject the idea of global warming or that they might be playing a part in it. Logically, they know better, but they're trapped in this one track, and they have the money and influence to continue to deny reality and to oppose a better way of doing things. But this particular track is heading for a wall.

The Dutch example shows that clever, designed policy can switch the points. The question is not if we can solve the problems; the question is whether we have the will to choose a prosperous and environmentally sound future.

THE TRUTH IS OUT THERE

It's obvious to any objective observer. Some smart corporations are starting to get ready for change, but most continue to steam along in their well-worn tracks. General Motors is probably an extreme example of a company that ignores everything but its own short-sighted view. For example, I remember a former chairman of the board, who also became chair of the board of the Nature Conservancy, a land-saving group, writing an article in the *Nature Conservancy News* about why sport utility vehicles (suvs) are central to the American purpose—because they make more profit. It was about as archaic a position as I can imagine, from what had been a much-respected environmental group. Now, in light of high gas prices and warnings throughout the media about global warming and the harm that is being done to our planet, largely from auto emissions, that position can be seen by all in a different light. Why would the Nature Conservancy publish such a view? Maybe it would become clear if we examine it from within a general time frame.

From a management ethics perspective, the Nature Conservancy story deserves a bit of a look. Basically, the normal, healthy management structure of complex institutions has a purposeful degree of stress built into it. In the U.S. government, for example, the courts are independent from Congress, which is supposed to be independent from the president. Each group can counter actions of the other. Thus, for an idea to move forward, there must be cooperation. That balance of power is also seen in most successful corporate structures, where the fiscal department is in balance with the marketing department, and both are overseen by the chief executive. In the nonprofit world, where organizations have to raise money—often from corporate sources—it takes balance to remain ethical and honest. The Nature Conservancy, for example, which is dedicated to protecting land, keeping it pristine and free from development, succumbed to corporate money, often from the very corporations whose influence on the land it was trying to offset—and, in my view, damaged its integrity in the process. That's a genuine loss. And I say that as someone who spent years helping to build the Nature Conservancy.

On the other hand, when cooperation works, as in the Dutch case, and the intention to protect the land is shared, both business and nonprofits can benefit from cooperation. In the Dutch case, the model has the stress built in. First of all, government gives long-term environmental interest a voice by defining the long-term ambitions and goals. The government negotiates and deals with industry, in order to change their former command-and-control procedures by working out some compromises. Then the environmental groups, the third party, or the third leg of a three-legged stool, keep tabs, growling at them, daring one of them to cheat or back out of their transactions. The role of the nonprofit is to communicate its observations to the media, which then communicates to the public. Public reporting and yearly independent assessments keep track of overall progress. Such assessments ensure transparency and accountability. So, in Holland, the economic interests are kept in balance with environmental interests.

In fact, in the Dutch case, the economic realm welcomed the intense guard-dog role of the environmental movement. When the Dutch started their Green Plan efforts, business leaders told me that this whole idea would evaporate in seconds if not for the aggressive guard-dog function of the environmental movement. The environmentalists watched and weighed and critically judged, and then transmitted their feelings to the public about whether policy changes were being overdone. That al-

lowed government and industry to do an honest job of negotiating with each other. They would reach a compromise, and
then pass it outside the room to the environmental group who
might accept it or might shriek and growl and send it off with
adamant opposition to the press.

DUTCH GOVERNMENT SUPPORT AND
ENVIRONMENTAL WATCHDOGS

Members of the Dutch industry that were negotiating—and not
all of them were involved—made a point of having government
give money to the nonprofit environmental activists, to make
sure they were vigorous and present. The idea was that those
who might wish to discontinue negotiating would be forced,
out of fear of the ferocious reaction of the environmentalists, to
stay and cooperate. This was an effective use of national policy,
which not all of industry welcomed. Some individual—often
smaller—companies were upset at that kind of negotiation. Before, they had been able to hire a group of lobbyists and get a
law passed that would benefit whatever narrow focused interest
they wanted. Now, they had to work in this larger arena, and
stay and cooperate. The environmentalists, in this case, were
setting a strong watchdog example.

As I've said, I write this from the vantage point of having
worked in industry, for nonprofits, and for government, at challenging levels. I worked for Union Carbide, I helped build the
Nature Conservancy, serving at one time as its national president, and I've been in government at a high policy level, responsible for California's environmental management. So my
views are based on an accumulation of satisfying experiences
in all three sectors. From my perspective, to compare the Dutch
model with the fossil fuel–dominated industrial mentality in the
United States should be food for thought for a lot of industrial
leaders and politicians.

The rest of the world is slowly pressing in and trying to force the United States to acknowledge our responsibilities but so far, despite the growing awareness of the seriousness of global warming and its consequences to the entire planet, the fossil-fuel interests in the United States prevail. But the successes of certain progressive state, town, and industry coalitions willing to meet Kyoto targets are chipping away at the limited vision of those who currently dominate U.S. policy.

The European Union, for example, is starting to show its emerging strength as an economic force in the world. They now require each new member to agree to serious environmental quality management procedures. Now, all of a sudden, those have popped up right in the lap of the American economy. In a move I'll discuss later in this book, the European Union has let Silicon Valley manufacturers know that they will not be allowed to export computers to Europe unless they comply with European standards regarding toxic materials used in their construction. Some companies will try to fight this, but others, such as Hewlett Packard, say they've been getting ready for this for some time. In the field of climate change, the EU has signed the Kyoto Protocol, divided the contribution to be made by each member state, and set up a system that enables the trading of emission rights.

So, in summary, we are in a state of change. If we relax and let time happen, now that other economic forces are emerging in the world, there is no escaping the trend. We can try to postpone it. We can continue upholding a false competitive advantage by selling out our environment and plundering our resources. Or we can invest in change and innovation and reap the benefits of action. Ultimately, if we design the framework for change wisely and negotiate with the aim of resolving the problems and balancing the interests of the whole against those of the special interests, the plan will work and everyone will welcome it. It will still require negotiation and dispute resolution—so that problems are resolved and all interests are balanced, not just those of vested interests. Remember: We can only solve *all of the problem* and to do that we need to manage *all the parts together*, at the same time. We have the tools we need to move forward with this kind of plan; what we need is the will to do it.

GREEN PLANS SHOW THE WAY

It seems that no one believes a project is doable until there are working models of success. The standard response from the "experts" is always: If that kind of approach worked, somebody would already be doing it. In the case of Green Plans, we can now answer that somebody is. A few comfortable, developed nations—ones that have traditionally been in the forefront of progressive social change—have begun to lead a global movement toward environmental recovery.

New Zealand was the first nation to give women the right to vote. The Netherlands was one of the first nations to institute child labor laws. These two nations and Singapore are now out in front of the rest of the world in solving the environmental problem. What they are doing is truly revolutionary; they have taken the position that a solution is not only possible but essential if we are to leave anything at all for future generations. Each of these countries has adopted its own comprehensive environmental policy, or Green Plan, a practical strategy designed to translate the concept of sustainability into action on the national and local levels. The Plan is not rigid, like a blueprint of societal development, but is a practical management tool to enable countries to resolve problems and galvanize all contributions to change. I believe that if the rest of the world would follow, with each nation developing its own innovations, the whole world would begin to see the beginnings of environmental recovery, and could imagine a return to environmental health.

There is a difference between musing about something and actually doing it, between thinking about what is possible and making those possibilities real. Throughout history there have been instances of revolutionary ideas that were pondered and discussed for years, building and building until some person or group finally brought them to life. Take the idea of human flight, for example. From the time of the ancient Greeks up until the early twentieth century, humans speculated and dreamed about the possibility of taking to the skies, but very few believed it would ever happen. Lindberg's flight changed the way we thought about human possibility.

The Green Plan idea is the beginning of another such leap. Like all new concepts it will go through many stages. Already, the Green Plan in action has become a remarkable achievement in the history of human accomplishment in free societies. The countries that are implementing Green Plans are the first in history to attempt to recover environmental quality nationwide. They have made environmental sustainability a key issue of national purpose. Like Lindberg, they are pushing humanity over the threshold into a new era.

At this writing, seven years into the twenty-first century, sustainability is at the point where Lindberg was in 1927, on the ground in New Jersey waiting for weather to clear to make his flight to Paris. Already, the Netherlands, New Zealand, and Singapore have let go of the safety line and moved from theory to practice, with all the inherent risks. Because they have taken the initiative and succeeded, the rest of the world will be able to benefit from their experience, observing their successes and setbacks, learning what works and what does not. I'm writing this third edition, twelve years after publication of the first book, to offer a very fine success model for the United States and other nations, showing not only what can be done but what *has* been done, and demonstrating clearly how successful planning is an essential tool for successful governance.

At this point, it would make no sense for any city, state, or nation to start from scratch in creating its own plan, because the level of thought and the degree of commitment that have gone into the plans of the Netherlands, Singapore, and New Zealand is so exemplary. Starting from scratch would cost many years and many millions of dollars, and it is unnecessary; we are not going to invent a better wheel. What these countries have done will be the models for others to follow and build upon. Each country will want to adapt its plan to its own circumstances, but the basic Green Plan design will be like that of the two-wheel bicycle; while individual bikes vary widely, the design principles followed by most have changed very little in the past century.

I will describe each of these three countries' Green Plans in detail in separate chapters and use examples from them to illustrate points throughout. It is important to keep in mind, however, that each country's plan is at a different stage of development. Because the Netherlands' plan was the first to be passed and is the most completely implemented so far, there is much more information available about it, and so its Green Plans play a larger role in this book. As I write this edition, New Zealand's plan is becoming a well-documented success as a working national policy.

The genius of Green Plans is that each of the of these pioneering countries' Green Plans is unique, taking into account each nation's distinctive characteristics and problems. While Holland is an industrial center, New Zealand is basically an agricultural export nation, and while their specific problems may be different, their goals—a healthy, sustainable environment—are the same. How does it work?

LIKE CLOCKWORK

Just as there are certain basic elements to a clock—the mainspring, the hands, the gears—there are certain elements basic to Green Plans. These are *comprehensiveness, integration, and a large-scale commitment by government and stakeholders.* Green Plans share other elements as well, primarily because they are examples of systems thinking—looking at whole systems rather than at discrete parts. The process of designing the comprehensive framework also has common process requirements: clear information, recognizing the critical contributions of many actors, and framing the policy debate in terms acceptable to all participants. Part 2 will cover some of these other elements in depth. The three "mainspring" elements, which constitute the definition of Green Plans as they have evolved to date, are discussed in detail below.

COMPREHENSIVENESS AND INTEGRATION

When we talk about the environment, we are not talking about just trees, or water, or air, but of all those things and more, interrelated in a very complex system. The ways in which we as humans interact with that system are equally complex: extracting resources, irrigating farmland, harvesting trees, burying our waste, creating energy. We cannot hope to remedy the effects we have had on the planet unless we develop policies that use this complexity as their starting point.

For some, the question will arise, Why go to all this trouble of shifting from simple single-issue concerns to the complex Green Plan? The answer is that those old ways are not working. A comprehensive approach works better for a list of reasons, not the least of which is managing costs and avoiding problems that are usually put off or shifted elsewhere. Above all, we have an obligation to future generations to keep the earth livable and productive. Our goal must be to fashion a healthy, sustainable society, one that is able to function within the limits set by nature.

In the past, our approaches to resource management and the environment in general have been fragmented. We did the best we could with the knowledge we had. Now we have new tools that enable us to access vast stores of complex information. I remember one of the world's eminent scientists, René Dubos, saying once that he doubted that humanity would ever be able to understand much more about ecology; it was too complex. He died before the computer had become the universal tool it is now. He could not have imagined the way the computer would enable scientists and even nonscientists to think through problems in seconds that might have taken months to review before.

Take forestry, for example. Most nations have traditionally been concerned solely with the economics of forestry. This means cutting trees, creating finished wood products, building homes and businesses, and carrying on trade. As forest resources rapidly depleted, some argued for the idea of harvesting trees in a sustainable manner. But this approach generally failed to take anything but trees into consideration. Then some regions realized that their fisheries were dying out, in part because silt from eroding clear-cut slopes had affected spawning streams. This discovery led to the realization that forestry and fisheries are linked.

We have also, in recent years, discovered links between forests and air pollution. The trees in some of the world's great forests, including Germany's Black Forest, are dying because of air pollution originating elsewhere. When the trees die, so do the songbirds and all the other life forms that depend on them, from microbes to elk. This has made us understand that if we want to have forests, we have to be concerned about the ways in which we are diminishing the quality of the air, from the toxins spewed from smokestacks to the exhaust belching from tailpipes. A third of the forests of Europe are suffering from the effects of air pollution, and it is increasingly affecting those of Canada and the United States.

FROM TAP WATER TO ENERGY POLICY

In the state of California, where I live, tap water is a factor in energy policy. It is also a factor in air pollution and a contributing cause of asthma. Why? Consider that when you turn on the tap, the water that pours out has traveled a long distance, through pipes, moved by great pumps driven by electricity, which is made by burning fossil fuel in the form of imported oil. How much impact does that have on California's energy use? According to the California Energy Commission's 2005 report, California's water infrastructure accounts for 20 percent of the state's energy consumption.[1] Electricity, generated by fossil fuel, is one of the largest sources of air pollution. Air pollution is associated with the rising number of cases of asthma. A 2006 American Lung Association report states that while mortality from asthma is currently not rising, asthma remains a major health concern. In 2004, the report states, approximately 20.5 million Americans had asthma. Asthma ranks in the top ten "prevalent conditions causing limitation of activity" and costs the nation approximately $16.1 billion annually.[2] Humans aren't the only ones affected by air pollution. Farms crops and forests are still suffering major damage by air pollution. All this new information about the interconnectedness of what had previously been considered separate issues provides strong basis for the idea of management change. Yet, while positive change is slowly happening, government efforts are still rarely organized to manage resources as a system; instead, they are typically fragmented between dozens of different agencies each dealing with a single issue. In order to survive, they engage in turf wars, fail to coordinate their policies, and fight over scraps of funding. Looking at a dozen agencies of government dealing with the environment—wildlife, parks, forestry, soil, water quality, and so on—reveals that they are rarely managed by one administrator, nor are they operated as a cohesive unit, functioning together the way a clock works. The examples in this book will show how the approach can be improved.

POWER AND POLITICS INFLUENCE CHOICE

Politics and power decide how various environmental issues are ranked. In most state or federal agencies in the United States today, agriculture, oil, and water are probably ranked at the top. Soil, wildlife, parks, and recreation get little attention or funding. The powerful agencies guard their privileged positions jealously, while the less powerful are left with the crumbs. They are fighting each other needlessly, and often none of them are managing their affairs very well.

When we leave behind an issue that is underfunded, like soil, we undermine all our efforts over the long term. We are wasting our money whenever we deal with forests and air quality and do not deal with the other issues. Often we are just pushing problems around from one realm to another, like sweeping trash under the rug, cleaning the water only to bury or incinerate the contaminants that have been removed. The result may clean the water, but pollute the air and soil.

The government of the Netherlands has put its finger on the problem very concisely: "The difficulty with this fragmented approach is that it addresses a succession of new issues without necessarily resolving the previous one, thereby creating the impression that it no longer matters. Attention focuses on one subject, overshadowing others, which are no less important. This approach also fails to treat the environment as a single system, which makes it virtually impossible to show people how their behavior affects the environment."[3]

In contrast, the Netherlands' comprehensive program has shown after eighteen years that its approach can make environmentally friendly behavior second nature to its people. Many of the original improvements of environmental practices have become a habit of Dutch citizens and are no longer problems. Sorting and recycling is something the thrifty and practical Dutch took to right at the start, as a way they could personally affect their environment. Now, through industrial ingenuity, the Dutch are transforming solid waste from a problem to a source of energy. Recycling is so much a part of their culture now that it is not even a subject of debate.

To achieve environmental recovery, we need to accept complexity. Green Plans are able to address complexity first of all because they are *comprehensive*, embracing all environmental and resource issues, across media and across geographical boundaries. Second, Green Plans are *integrated* throughout human society as it relates to the environment, from industry and government to social groups and individuals. Green Plans look at the interconnections and relationships between different environmental issues and between natural and human systems, and create similar links between those responsible for creating and implementing environmental policies. People working together combine experiences. Management that brings people and experience together is more effective than the old, adversarial methods. Comprehensive, integrated approaches to environmental planning bring cohesiveness to government efforts and encourage coordination and cooperation. They also make government and the management of environmental quality understandable and sensible to the public.

The Green Plans of the Netherlands, New Zealand, and Singapore are comprehensive, ecosystem-based initiatives designed to save the forest, not just the trees. Instead of passing laws that attack each problem one by one in isolation, these countries, in order to achieve their agreed-upon, long-term environmental goals, have created approaches that cut across traditional lines in ways that make sense for their resources, population, and industry. Within government itself, they have pulled together all the major ministries and agencies into one coordinated effort to achieve environmental quality.

Implementing such plans is obviously a challenge for each country. However, their comprehensiveness has in some ways made implementation easier, allowing all three nations to move away from the layering of regulatory and legal approaches that had developed over the years. They have replaced this old system with a refined, more efficient, broad strategy that gives businesses and individuals greater latitude within their organizations to meet and maintain the environmental goals they've helped to set. This means far less frustration, particularly for businesses that have tried to cooperate in the past, only to become mired in overlapping or outdated regulations, with their knowledge about clever solutions largely untapped.

An important element in this sort of comprehensive planning is a process for bringing together all interested groups, including environmentalists, industry, and citizens, to carefully review existing laws and regulations and develop a new more cooperative approach. The objectives of the plan must be clearly established and the goals clearly defined. Once that is done, it is no longer necessary to pile regulation on top of regulation.

It is interesting to compare what is happening in these three countries with the policies of California, a state that has a reputation for being modern and efficient, and which has adopted strong, farsighted policies on a number of environmental issues. For example, California led the alternative energy revolution, and as a consequence the state has a steady stream of visitors from all over the world who come to study its energy efficiency model. It also has strict air quality standards. But because California has not made the leap to the broader, comprehensive approach, its policies in other areas are severely lacking. The state's water policy is backward and poorly managed, and soil policies scarcely exist at this point. A sordid example is that of dry, desert communities using fossil water, that is, underground aquifers, that don't recharge each year but only continue to decline. I visited one recently in Borrega Springs, where no one was allowed to measure the extent to which underground water supplies had become limited. And the larger town of Palm Springs now has over one hundred golf courses, all operating by pumping water from underground aquifers that do not recharge. In time, the town and its golf courses will go back to desert. Rapid transit and growth policies are similarly short-sighted. Until California links its policy and regulatory programs together, it will not come close to providing a livable future for its citizens. Yet if the state were able to set a worldwide example on energy policy, it may not be too rash to think that, building on that experience, it would set a nationwide example of comprehensive environmental planning.

Environmental strategies for the future will have to be comprehensive in order to cope with the complexity of the environment and of the problems we face. Comprehensive plans will *work*, because they have the power of mass behind them. As I have said, the environmental idea has a better chance of success if it is part of a larger whole; single issues are far easier to block or defeat. And with fair contributions from everyone there is a critical mass to resolve the problems.

A LARGE-SCALE COMMITMENT BY GOVERNMENT

The other critical element of a Green Plan is its scale. The size and scale of the project must match that of the problem. In the United States, that would include federal, regional, and local governments. In the past, we have not really comprehended just how big and complex environmental problems are, so we have not responded appropriately—and for problems that are best solved at the federal level, we have even backed away.

Scale is one reason that Green Plans place responsibility for environmental planning at the national or state level. The way our system works only government can manage something of this size efficiently and effectively. For instance, consider the amount of money that is required—billions. In the case of existing national plans, this is far beyond what an organization or institution at the state level would be able to provide.

There are other Green Plan functions that only government can do, such as managing the taxes and environmental quality regulations, and enforcing the laws. Only government has the resources and the scope required to handle a project this immense. If it is efficiently run, the government has a tremendous advantage when it comes to the delivery of certain services. It does not mean that all problems have to be solved at the highest level. Local and regional problems should be dealt with at their respective levels. But the effectiveness of policy will increase if these efforts are part of a more comprehensive framework. Otherwise, when one country cleans up its river, but a country upstream of it does not, the pollution from the upstream country will continue to pollute the rest of the river downstream. This happened to Holland when they cleaned up their portion of the Rhine River, while the countries upstream from them did not. Now, with policy improvements affecting whole regions, the Rhine is remarkably improved and the salmon are back in the river.

In the United States in the last few decades, it has become fashionable to think that government is useless and that only private enterprise can handle problems efficiently. But it is a mistake to view the two as necessarily opposed. Privatization can be an important part of the way a government functions, but it should not be seen as a panacea that necessarily does a better job than the government or absolves the government of responsibility. For example, it may be most efficient to have a private firm collect a city's trash, but it is still the government's responsibility to make sure that the trash *is* picked up and disposed of properly. So while Green Plans may well include roles for private enterprise, they will require, first and foremost, government leadership and commitment to define the goals to be achieved and to safeguard the qualities of life we all value. They will have to preserve public goods and services and craft the framework for change—not as a body that is producing red tape and bureaucratic rules, but one that delivers on crucial issues we all value: health, nature, and security.

LESSONS ALREADY LEARNED

One lesson we have learned over the last ten years is that, given a chance, government agencies tend to revert back to a part-by-part approach at the expense of the whole program if not given firm oversight by an administration responsible for the whole.

We have always underestimated the environmental problem, but we come closer to understanding its size and scale when we see the size and scale of the response from a nation like the Netherlands. The Netherlands' Green Plan is an example of technical excellence, a multifaceted and detailed approach. To achieve its goal of recovering environmental quality in twenty-five years, the government has enlisted hundreds of people, including some of the country's best minds, in the task.

What happened in the Netherlands reminds me of the preparation for the Normandy invasion during World War II. I remember well the pictures of thousands of ships sitting offshore—the largest armada in history, all coordinated, all waiting to act in concert. It is that kind of human endeavor that a nation undertakes with these Green Plans: a massive commitment to a purpose.

Looking back in U.S. history for a comparison, perhaps the best is that of the soil conservation effort intended to stop wind erosion of the Great Plains at the end of the Depression. For a very short time, soil was understood as the key to a nation's survival, and great passion went into the effort to save the Plains from devastation. But the effort was not maintained over the years, and in any case fell short of what was needed.

The scale of our *funding* commitment has to match the size of the problem, too. We have a habit of putting a symbolic amount toward an issue, rather than enough to really have an effect. In trying to determine whether an institution is committed to a particular policy, one of the best questions to ask is what portion of the total amount it spends is devoted to implementing that policy. A government or corporation can say that it has the best health program in the world, but if it has yet to commit any money, then all it has is a piece of paper, not a program.

Using this measure, the Singapore example is quite remarkable. At a time when its economy was battered by recession, the Singapore government pledged to support the plan. It is still going strong.[4] The Canadian example was based on spending several billion dollars for government to distribute, but without requiring citizen involvement. The result was that when the money was spent there was no political basis for continuation. The next head of government ignored it, and since the public was not involved, they didn't challenge him to keep it going. They did in the New Zealand case, which I describe later.

In the past, we have rarely been able to think far enough ahead to fund a project adequately. As a result, we often end up wasting money and falling short of our goals. Soil cleanup efforts from across the world provide good examples. Had we been wise enough and willing enough to prevent soil contamination in the first place it would have been ten to twenty times cheaper to prevent the problem than to clean it up later.

PUTTING IT TOGETHER

If a national environmental recovery strategy is to be successful, it must incorporate and build upon the three main principles of comprehensiveness, integration, and a large-scale commitment by government. The precise methods used to implement each of these principles will be different for each nation, and will probably change over time, but a program that fails to include any one of them will not be a true Green Plan.

The examples provided by the Netherlands, New Zealand, and Singapore are especially important now that the world is shifting into a new phase in environmental planning. The adoption of a resolution entitled Agenda 21, signed by more than 170 nations attending the United Nations' Earth Summit in Rio in 1992, indicates widespread recognition that our old ways of responding to environmental problems are no longer sufficient.[5] By adopting Agenda 21, those nations agreed to follow a comprehensive, integrated, Green Plan approach to managing their environmental affairs. The pioneer Green Plans I describe in the following chapters are extremely useful models for the nations now starting down this track.

| Sustainability
A Modern Odyssey

WHAT'S IN A WORD?

Experts who are paid to define ideas are always searching for the exact phrase or word that reaches into the essence of a product or an idea, so that everyone hearing it knows exactly what is meant, with all the nuances and associations. The fact that everybody gets it creates a culture of shared understanding around that term—"Mac," for example, or "Martha Stewart." The right words, on packages or billboards or in speech, have the power to draw people together in a common understanding, or behind a common idea.

A friend of mine, Yvon Chouinard, started a company in the United States that sold climbing equipment, which he called Chouinard Equipment. One day he was mountain climbing with some Scottish climbers and noticed they had on big rugby shirts and that their arms were not getting bruised or scratched. Liking the style and function, he took some shirts back with

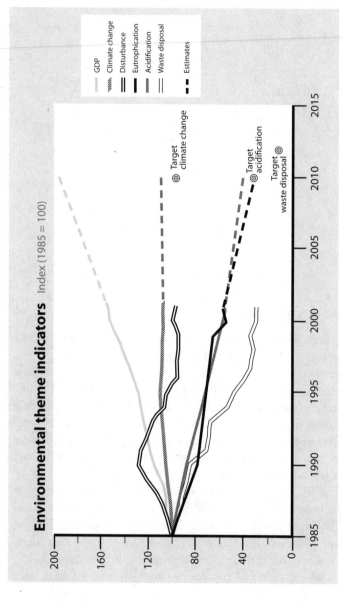

Environmental theme indicators Index (1985 = 100)

Legend:
- GDP
- Climate change
- Disturbance
- Eutrophication
- Acidification
- Waste disposal
- Estimates

Target climate change

Target acidification

Target waste disposal

Fig. 1. Environmental theme indicators, 1985

him and applied his little label, "Patagonia," and a marketing phenomenon was born. When you look at the label, you feel the far-off mountain air, when you put on the jacket, you put on a whole idea.

The environmental movement has its own "Patagonia" story. It happened back in 1987. The UN's World Commission on Environment and Development was about to deliver a blunt message about the perilous state of the global environment and wanted to call the citizens of the world to unite in the effort of averting environmental disaster. As they prepared the document, *Our Common Future*—which became known simply as the Brundtland Report, after the commission's chair, former Norwegian prime minister Gro Harlem Brundtland—they searched for a term that would sum up in one memorable word or phrase the change everyone needed to rally around. The term they came up with, and which is now used around the world, is *sustainable development*.

WHAT IS SUSTAINABLE DEVELOPMENT?

Although the concept has been a subject of academic study for decades, the Brundtland Report emphasized the links between problems of growth, economics, technology, and the environment, and defined sustainability as "development that meets the needs of the present without compromising the ability of future generations to meet their own needs."

Ever since the Brundtland Report was published, the concept of sustainable development has been widely discussed and debated. The report itself, and the debates it inspired, gave shape and impetus to the Green Plan idea in the countries that are now adopting it. As a rallying cry, sustainable development has defined the hope that if we pursued the right avenues we could make a positive change. As a negotiating tool, it has served to enable people of opposing sides to approach discussing the common problem without alienating each other. All Green Plans have the ultimate goal of achieving sustainable development, but though the term itself has served an important philosophical and social purpose, as a definition, it is imprecise.

LIMITS TO THE DISCUSSION OF LIMITS

Although it would be realistic to discuss the topic of growth from a limits perspective, the influential voices from the world of economics would rise up and object to the threat of limits. This brings up an interesting point: One of the admirable qualities of the human condition is that when things seem to get really bogged down, diplomats seem to be able to get together and end a war. In this case, in the midst of violent opposition on the part of the various interests, the word *sustainability* surfaced and became a means of shifting gears into a more rational discussion. The term played a pacifying role. Whereas economists went crazy over the idea of "limits," as insisted upon in the "limits to growth" books, *sustainability* was a safe-sounding word—more permissive than limits—and it was immediately embraced. Who could object to sustainability? The question remains: What does it mean, in terms of a practical definition?

The term has had the simultaneous advantage and disadvantage of being vague enough to allow a multitude of definitions—which meant more people could embrace it without feeling threatened—but also imprecise enough to leave the door open for genuine misunderstanding over what the concept really involves. As a result, the term *sustainable development* has almost become a buzzword, often put forth as the solution to humanity's problems but rarely accompanied by any explanation or definition of how it is to be accomplished. This vagueness, where it allows for initial wide acceptance of the perceived idea, can create unfortunate consequences at the implementation stage.

For example, one of the world's original leaders on Green Plans, whom I interviewed seven years ago, recently told me why he believes the Canadian Green Plan came to an early end. The plan had started out with inspiring energy, and they were in the crucial process of working out the long conflict between economic and environmental interests. Then some social activists decided that Green Plans needed to stretch out and include a social dimension, such as education, health care, or prison reform. I've seen this happen often with successful programs in government—everybody tries to throw their idea on the wagon until the wagon can't move. So, sad but true, that's what happened to the Green Plan in Canada. Instead of a smooth ongoing exchange between the two parties—government and industry—monitored by the environmental watchdogs, a third interest, dedicated to solving social concerns, was introduced into the negotiations with the result that the balance was upset and some of the influential voices from both the economic and environmental sides abandoned the table, as well as the idea. Then the whole thing fell apart.

While this may seem to be a cautionary tale, I will add that it is obvious to me that there is an additional dimension to the environmental problem, and that is health. Health problems are the inescapable consequence of environmental degradation. I don't see this as an additional issue, but an integral part of the environmental problem. Had negotiations included this aspect from the beginning, they could well have worked. The problem with Canada was that they loaded on a pile of new concerns, and they did it midstream, upsetting the delicate balance necessary for any negotiation. Clearer terminology at the start could have helped prevent that.

A ROSE BY ANY OTHER NAME

Despite the debate over terminology and application, sustainable development is now the fairly universal term we use when discussing our concerns about environmental decline and our hopes and plans for change. The universality of the term is less a tribute to its evocative ring than it is an acknowledgment of the obviousness of the need and the programs to which it refers. You could have named it "green tomatoes" and the world would have embraced it. To date, none of the attempts to refine the concept we call sustainable development has improved on Brundtland's original definition: the ability to meet current needs without compromising the ability of future generations to meet theirs. And while we might imagine more poetic phrases, sustainable development is still the workhorse phrase that has laid down a philosophical basis for delivering hope to the future.

A BRIEF HISTORY OF SUSTAINABLE DEVELOPMENT

Since the famous Brundtland Report, the idea of sustainable development has changed the way we think about and interact with the environment. Therefore, it is important to understand where this idea came from and where it is leading us, as well as to look at how existing Green Plans are adapting it to fill the gap between theory and practice.

Although a century earlier Thoreau, Marsh, Muir, and Leopold were concerned about what we would now call ecological sustainability, current thinking about the subject has its roots in the 1960s and 1970s, when the exponential growth of human population and the pressures it was putting on the natural environment began to set off alarms. In 1969, when Apollo 8 sent back the first full picture of the earth from space, we suddenly could see for ourselves this small globe in the vastness of the universe. We could see that the world we personally experience as limitless has finite resources and a finite ability to absorb the effects of our human activities. Some scientists began to be concerned that we might fast be approaching the limits of what the earth could support. Reports began to appear detailing the results of scientific studies on the ultimate effects of growth on the planet. Some proposed that we humans, in addition to adopting population control measures, needed to change our economic activities if we were to avoid environmental and economic disaster. Some worried that our poor understanding of the effects of our activities, and the inevitable time lag in responding to environmental crises, would cause us to do permanent damage to the earth's carrying capacity, or its ability to sustain us into the future.

All of these early studies, from the scientific to the popular, urged some form of rapid self-imposed limits to growth, both in population and in economic activity. In 1972, *The Limits to Growth*, the MIT study commissioned by the Club of Rome, recommended a number of measures designed to achieve an "equilibrium state" between resources, population, production, and consumption. In 1973, Fritz Schumacher, in his book *Small Is Beautiful*, motivated a great number of experiments in human habitation and resource use and revolutionized the way we thought about those resources that we take for granted. Paul and Anne Ehrlich, in their 1977 book *Population, Resources, Environments: Issues in Human Ecology*, recommended "de-development" for developed countries and a new type of semidevelopment for underdeveloped countries. In 1980, former West German chancellor Willy Brandt, in his book *North-South: A Programme for Survival*, delivered a stark warning about the consequences of the increasing inequity between developed and underdeveloped nations and recommended that the north, or industrial nations, actually tax themselves to create a fund for the developing nations. He also called for a worldwide change from oil to renewable energy sources, and recommended that ecological sustainability become central to global economic policy. All of these writers agreed that a more equitable distribution of wealth and resources between developed and underdeveloped countries would have to occur if environmental health, as we understand it, were to be preserved.

Efforts to unite the world leaders in a concerted effort

to work toward sustainable development continued. First there was the 1972 Conference on the Human Environment in Stockholm, from which came the UN Environmental Programme and later the work of the Brundtland Commission. Then, at the Earth Summit in Rio, in 1992, 170 nations committed themselves to sustainable development as a principle for future national and international actions, setting the environmental agenda for the next century. Former president George H. W. Bush, representing the United States, declined to join the other nations, stating that the American way of life was not up for compromise.

In 2002, nations again gathered, this time in Johannesburg, for the World Summit on Sustainable Development. The first goal was to encourage nations to fulfill their commitments made in Rio, ten years earlier. Some of the other goals included having industrial nations take the lead in promoting sustainable practices, promote implementation of the "polluter pays" principal, focus on youth, incorporate product life-cycle analysis into policy, develop cleaner fuel, and others.

HOW SUSTAINABLE IS SUSTAINABLE DEVELOPMENT?

In 1987 the Brundtland Report acknowledged that the world could not support the continued growth of *current* economic practices, but rejected the idea that growth itself is necessarily unsustainable. The report argued that a certain amount of growth is essential, particularly in the developing nations, and that the integration of environmental and economic considerations in human decision-making processes could lead to greater efficiencies in resource use and to intelligent, equitable economic growth. While few challenge the Brundtland Report's assessment that development must occur and standards of living must be raised in underdeveloped nations, there remains significant opposition to the idea that quantitative economic growth can be sustainable.

Herman Daly, an environmental economist (often described as a maverick or "eco-visionary") working as a senior economist for the World Bank in the mid-1980s, holds that sustainable growth within a finite ecosystem is an oxymoron. Even sustainable *development*, at the level recommended in the Brundtland Report, is pushing the limits of the earth's capacity because, he argues, "the natural world we live in has physical limits, so must the physical dimensions of our production and consumption of goods. Consequently growth should refer to quantitative expansion in the scale of the physical dimensions of the economic system, while 'development' should refer to the qualitative change of a physically non-growing economic system in dynamic equilibrium with the environment."[1]

To those who complain that limiting growth is damaging to economic health, he holds the revolutionary view that economy should be considered *within* ecological concerns, not the other way around, as the fossil fuel–based industries typically practice. He left the World Bank with a few choice parting shots, advising that they get glasses and hearing aids and basically wake up to what's happening. In an invited address to the World Bank in 2002, Daly warned: "Growth in GDP has begun to increase environmental and social costs faster than it increases production benefits. Such uneconomic growth makes us poorer, not richer."[2] He now teaches at the University of Maryland's Institute for Philosophy and Public Policy (as the Economics Department, he wryly notes, wouldn't have him).

Daly argues throughout his writings that continued economic growth does not necessarily contribute to people's well being, economic or otherwise, while it inevitably diminishes the earth's "natural capital," or ability to provide humans with goods and services. His view is that that current economic theory is based on a false picture of what humans are and how they act; that it is an abstraction that relies too heavily on market transactions and income as measures of well-being. Daly's theories have not been welcomed by traditional economists, but his work and that of others has had some impact on the international policy debate. Whether economic *growth* can or should be sustainable is a question likely to be argued far into the future.

SOME REALITIES OF RESOURCE CONSUMPTION AND SUSTAINABILITY

The idea of moving toward equity in resource consumption is central to Brundtland's and others' definitions of sustainable development, most of which attempt to resolve the historic problem of industrialized nations appropriating the resources of southern hemisphere nations. The current reality is, despite all warnings from those I've just mentioned, among others, the industrialized nations continue to consume far more than their share of resources. According to Worldwatch Institute's *Vital Signs 2003*, humanity is using resources 20 percent faster than the earth can renew them, and is consequently depleting the resources on which our survival depends.[3]

IT'S A WAR AND PEACE ISSUE

While flying to Oslo, Norway, as a guest of the 2004 winner of the Nobel Peace Prize, environmentalist Dr. Wangari Maathai, I took advantage of the time away from ringing phones and mused upon the revolutionary event I was about to witness: the Nobel Peace Prize awarded, for the first time ever, for environmental work. This acknowledgement of the inextricable connection between peace and environment expands forever the parameters of what we think of as "environmentalism." It's not about hugging trees, or even, as Dr. Maathai is being honored for, planting trees. It is about the survival of societies, about war and peace. As Dr. Maathai commented in her acceptance speech: "There can be no peace without equitable development;

and there can be no development without sustainable management of the environment in a democratic and peaceful space. This shift is an idea whose time has come."

History agrees. It shows us that wars can generally be tracked to a shortage of resources. One nation runs out of iron ore or coal—which is the story of Germany and France and two world wars—another runs out of water, which is the subtext of the current civil war in Sudan. If we wonder why we should be concerned, as these events are far removed in time and geography, we would do well to remember that history repeats itself. While some achieve benefit from war, when we get into a state of world wars, it isn't beneficial to anyone. In the end, because of the devastation and cost and suffering, it could be argued that we should never go in the direction of war again. As the wild consumption continues on one hand, and tragic poverty continues on the other, the imbalance goes deeper, and the poorest of the poor have no reasons to care about environment or anything else. So you end up with suicide bombers.

The Roman Empire, for example, grew their grain in North Africa. When they exhausted the productivity of these fields by too much irrigation and the resulting salinity killed the wheat, people suddenly didn't have any bread, and they rioted. The nation came apart at the seams. So we have that condition repeated in history. There are other examples, but the main thing is that it is a human legacy. As we observed from the space shot, we can see that the earth is really a rather small place and it's stressed increasingly by our mismanagement of it. Wars will occur as a result of environmental collapse or ecological ruin. That's why the EU is working so well, for both economic and ecological health.

TO LEAVE A LIGHTER FOOTPRINT ON THE EARTH

As time passes, new dimensions to the idea of sustainability have evolved. For example, a California group called Redefining Progress uses the term *ecological footprint* to show in concrete terms, both to individuals and whole communities, what their impact is on the environment.[4] You may think you're conducting an ecologically conscious life, for example, but if you take their little quiz, you may find that your "ecological footprint" is way too big for what your portion of the earth can sustain. So you find that you are part of the problem. What is to be done?

The equity issue is further complicated by the fact that the earth's diminishing pool of resources simply cannot support such high resource consumption in the underdeveloped nations or by future generations. Unless the industrialized nations cut back their use of resources, others cannot hope for much improvement in their standards of living. It is clear that if we continue to follow current practices, we will create an environmental legacy that will reduce the standard of living for *everyone* in the future, and cause increasing human suffering and conflict as well.

The concept of sustainable development defines the problem, but what are the solutions? How does one nation adopt a policy or policies that adequately address issues of a global nature? A nation's answers will differ greatly depending on whether it is developed or developing and how it perceives its need.

Currently, in many nations, especially in the United States, the desire to maintain an economic boom outweighs the need to account for the real cost of our industrial lifestyle. A realistic appraisal of our ecological footprint can encourage environmentally sound practices, from choosing fuel efficient automobiles to using green architectural standards to designing for energy conservation in buildings. In essence, the experience of the Netherlands, New Zealand, and Singapore can show the world's free societies how to balance resources with desires—with sustainability as the goal. Our unwillingness to consider such planning is beginning to cost the United States, as we can see in the loss of value of the dollar against the euro. In fact, sustainability conscious Europe is economically thriving. The EU is the most dramatic advance in the importance of planning since the last edition of this book, as I will discuss further on. As a matter of note: as of June, 2006, the EU has published on their Web site a detailed and comprehensive policy statement on sustainable development. It describes sustainable development as offering "a vision of progress that integrates immediate and long-term needs, local and global needs, and regards social, economic, and environmental needs as inseparable and interdependent components of human progress." It cautions that sustainable development cannot be achieved by policy statements alone, but must be embraced by society as a whole. The complete statement is available on the EU Web site at http://ec.europa.eu/environment/eussd along with an October 2007 Progress Report.

THE ECONOMIC SUCCESS OF GREEN PLANNING

As the discussion of sustainable development among industrialized nations has focused on the unsustainable practices of developing countries, many of which are driven by poverty and the desperate need for economic growth, many in the developed countries tend to forget that developed countries not only consume the most resources but are also the source of most environmental problems.

In writing this book I've emphasized several small countries, which successfully use a Green Plan, and the twenty-seven-nation European Union, which is also experiencing successful, comprehensive environmental change. However, such forward-thinking success is threatened to be offset by the old line, simple economic, large-scale industrial development that is happening in China and India. While both are enjoying short-term economic growth benefits and a huge improvement in life quality for much of the country, the old specter of environmental degradation, especially of air and water, emerges—but this time in such large scale as to be threatening to global stability.

For instance, with the recent burst of automobile ownership, air quality is becoming an issue in Beijing. On bad air days one can't see far or breathe comfortably. An error in land use and water management has resulted in one-third of the agricultural lands having been given over to supply new factories. I chaired a panel in Beijing a year ago, which included China's minister for environment and population. He admitted that up to one-third of China's agricultural lands have recently been taken out of production in order to use the water to build and run more factories. Why? They provide more jobs. It was not that he was happy about it; he was, as usually happens, just outweighed by economic advocates.

As a partner in world trade, the United States shares responsibility for the dilemma of the imminent problem in Asia. No one seems concerned about the long-term effects of environmental decline. These comments about China are my own observations, but I'm optimistic too. Because of its ability to accept governance, I believe it is one of the few nations that can successfully regroup, manage its environmental problems, and still grow. Already, its standards for automobile fuel efficiency put ours to shame.

Developed countries need to get their own houses in order, adopting rational, comprehensive policies that will make their resource use more efficient and clean up their messes, before they can expect to be very effective at telling others how they should manage their affairs. Developing countries are not going to respect demands that they take better care of their resources unless developed nations first show that they are serious about doing their part. Until they do so, the underdeveloped countries have every reason to be apprehensive about either the intent of the developed nations or their intelligence.

This does not mean that developed countries should ignore global questions. Pursuing courses toward the sustainable use of their own resources does not mean that they will stop pursuing international agreements or providing financial and technical aid to the developing countries. Developed nations must also be prepared to share information and technology relevant to sustainability.

Developing countries will benefit in any case from this approach. New efficiencies practiced by developed nations will free up resources for use in the developing world. In addition, the pioneering work of industrialized countries will develop a body of experience that should prove useful to the underdeveloped nations as they begin to create their own plans. It will allow them to study and evaluate what has already been done, and to think about which approaches might be best for their own planning.

Brundtland's concept of sustainable development is a philosophical statement, not an action plan—though it has been misinterpreted as such. In fact, the Dutch initially attempted to use the Brundtland definition to pursue sustainable development. It didn't work, and they prepared their own approach, the Green Plan.

Governments that have developed Green Plans understand the distinction well; while they have adopted the principle of sustainable development as their ultimate goal, they have also forged ahead with more refined definitions and action plans regarding the sustainability of their own resource base. By applying the concept of sustainable development in the real world, they are defining it as they go.

GREEN PLANS IN ACTION

The rest of this chapter will look at how two of the three main Green Plan countries are dealing with the sustainability question on a practical level. Each has taken a somewhat different approach, tailored to fit their differing environmental problems and social characteristics. New Zealand's approach is primarily structural, rethinking its environmental laws and governmental structure so that both are now directed toward the principle of sustainability. The Netherlands, with its higher level of environmental problems, has chosen a technical interpretation of sustainability, aiming to recover a high level of environmental quality within twenty-five years.

NEW ZEALAND'S SUSTAINABLE MANAGEMENT

When New Zealand was going through the process of creating a new resource management policy, the debate in parliament over the real meaning of sustainable development was thoughtful and drawn-out. By about midnight, when they were still unable to reach any agreement, an elder senator in opposition was asked what he would require to support the legislation. He said they should stop trying to make it a cure-all for all the social problems of New Zealand and accept that what they wanted was improved resource management that would be sustainable over time.

They adopted the term *sustainable management* to describe what they wanted their new legislation to accomplish. Their definition of the term can be summarized as "managing the use, development, and protection of natural and physical resources in a way, or at a rate, which enables people to meet their needs now without compromising the ability of future generations to meet their own needs."

Sustainable management, as the New Zealanders see it, is their route to achieving sustainable development as defined by Brundtland, but is a more accurate description of how they will apply it to their own unique environment and economy. They are well aware of the international responsibilities of sustainable development and know that international goals cannot be achieved without first meeting national ones. They are cleaning their own house first.

Decision making within New Zealand's concept of sustainable management involves a range of environmental protections. At one end of the scale are environmental "bottom lines," which are points beyond which a resource or ecosystem will risk suffering irreversible effects. These bottom lines represent the minimum of environmental protection in New Zealand; ideally, no decisions will be made that would allow a system to go below this line. There have been some new directions and adjustments to the program, which is to be expected. Over time, any of these programs could require adjustments, take new directions, or retreat from former ones, as I will describe in chapter 6.

At the other end of the scale are points beyond which no modification occurs whatsoever, cases in which ecosystems or areas will effectively be set aside and no direct human influence allowed. In between these two points are areas in which decision makers will have to weigh environmental, economic, and social concerns. Within these parameters they hope to establish standards that will define sustainability across the environmental spectrum.

Sustainable management is neither anti- nor pro-development; it is only concerned with the effects and potential effects of development on the environment's sustainability. New Zealanders believe that a distinction must not be made between development and the environment; in other words, development must fit into the framework of sustainable management of resources. Although they think it is possible to have development and growth, they realize that there must be conditions placed upon it to ensure sustainability.

THE NETHERLANDS' TECHNICAL APPROACH

The Dutch spend very little time talking about sustainable development, but it is nonetheless the guiding principle of their environmental policies. Although they had been moving in the direction of a more comprehensive environmental policy before the Brundtland Report, their Green Plan, the National Environmental Policy Plan (NEPP), was to a large extent a response to Brundtland. Their program has been described in different ways, but one is as a social contract, an informal cooperative agreement between industry, government, and the private sector over the objectives of their Green Plan.

The Dutch have chosen to focus on Brundtland's appeal that nations stop shifting responsibility for environmental problems onto future generations and other countries. That is why they have set themselves the goal of recovering the Netherlands' environmental quality in one generation. In working toward that goal they are trying to manage their ecological footprint ethically. For instance they now prohibit shipping their wastes to other nations. They also use the idea of equity for future generations to inspire their people to make environmentally sound decisions.

Overall, the Dutch define sustainability for their own country in terms of reducing emissions and reversing unacceptable practices in each of their environmental problem areas (which they call "themes") to such an extent that the environment can continue to function at an acceptable level in the future. With the help of independent scientists, they have already determined the reductions required in each problem area and for each "target group" that contributes to those problems. They are in the process of developing sustainability indicators—instruments to help them track their progress for all the themes, and publish an annual report of the sustainability performance of major Dutch companies—available so far, only in Dutch.

Sustainability, the Dutch believe, must be pursued by "feedback mechanisms" aimed at the sources of environmental deterioration. These feedback mechanisms focus on the proper management of material and energy flows. They are: integrated cycle management (closing material cycles in the chain from raw material to production process to product to waste, to eliminate leaks); quality promotion (improving the quality, rather than increasing the quantity, of raw materials, production processes, and products); and reduction of energy use. Attention must be focused on all three of these elements simultaneously, the Dutch believe, if sustainability is to be achieved. It is interesting to note that, in the four-year report on their plan, they anticipate that even more fundamental changes may be necessary if they are going to achieve genuine sustainability.

Now, once again demonstrating the excellence of the Dutch planning, preparation, and commitment to public information, they have pulled together a summary of all their activities that relate to their goal of sustainability. The report is titled, "Sustainable Development Action Programme Progress Report, 2004." This report is available to be downloaded from: http//www.vrom.nl.

AGENDA 21

The experiences of the New Zealanders, Singaporeans, and the Dutch show that the idea of sustainable development can be adapted and refined in various ways to make it a useful theoretical tool, from the national level on down to the local. The theme of sustainability will be repeated in one form or another, as both developed and developing nations create Green Plans.

In the international community, where sustainable development has been discussed and debated ever since the Brundtland Report, the idea is gaining ground. At the 1992 Earth Summit in Rio, 170 nations agreed to Agenda 21, which promotes cooperation on environmental recovery through the principles of sustainable development. Like the Green Plan idea, Agenda 21 grew out of the Brundtland Report and its concept of sustainable development. Thus, it is no surprise that the two share some of the same principles and management strategies, the most important of which are the integration of economics and environment into decision making on all levels, and a comprehensive approach to resource management.

Agenda 21 is not itself a Green Plan, but rather an agreement on sustainability as a common goal for the nations of the world and a framework for international cooperation toward it. In that context, it urges all countries to adopt national strategies for sustainable development—in essence, Green Plans. In addition, the UN Development Programme has announced a new department within the UN that will aid developing countries in implementing Green Plans of their own.

Agenda 21 is already having a major impact in the world. For example, the annual report of New Zealand's Ministry for Environment to its House of Representatives declares that one of the ministry's objectives is to work with other departments, local governments, industry, and community groups to ensure that the programs of Agenda 21 are incorporated into making policy and decisions. New Zealand is one of the first nations to move ahead with fulfilling its obligations under the agreement. Increasingly one is seeing versions of Agenda 21 on the local level as well. The Rio agreement particularly emphasized the desirability of having communities develop their own comprehensive strategies for managing their affairs sustainably.

SUSTAINABILITY AND THE FUTURE OF THE WORLD

What does sustainable development really mean for the future of the world? It all comes down to this: The earth has a certain capacity, and to be able to manage it in an environmentally as well as economically friendly way we will, in the end, have to make some choices about how much we are going to produce and how much we are going to consume, and about the ways in which we produce and consume. That also means dealing with a related issue—one that is hard to discuss even in the United States—population growth.

When exponential population growth and the poverty it is linked to were confined to the underdeveloped world, the developed nations believed they could ignore the issue. But another outgrowth of overpopulation and poverty, namely mass migration, has made this increasingly difficult. Mass migrations of people from nations in the underdeveloped world, and from rural areas to the cities in some large nations, are becoming more and more common, and as the world grows smaller, travel will become easier even for those who have no money. There will be growing pressure on the Western world from the south and from eastern countries in Europe. Worldwatch Institute estimates that within the next fifty years some 150 million people may have fled areas vulnerable to rising sea levels or failing agricultural productivity into cities or across borders.

Mass migration not only overburdens the areas people are moving to, but often further impoverishes the areas they came from as well. The solution most often overlooked is to make social and economic life better for the citizens of countries at the source of the migration. In order to do this, the developed nations will have to keep a tight rein on the size of their own populations and become much more efficient in their use of resources, because each citizen of a developed nation consumes a much higher proportion of resources. Developed countries will also have to help the developing countries improve their use of resources while at the same time lessening the pressure on the environment. All this will require greater resource efficiency and different ways of producing and consuming.

For example, China has a population of 1.3 billion people, or 21 percent of the earth's population, but has only 10 percent of the world's arable land and 25 percent of the world's water resources per person. In the last twenty-five years, the pace of economic growth in China has averaged over 9.5 percent. According to figures provided by the Organisation for Economic Co-operation and Development (OECD), the size of the economy now exceeds a number of major European economies. This progress began in the agricultural sector twenty years ago and has been driven by changes in the government's economic policy. The result has been a rise in income, even in rural areas, and a rise in environmental pollution. According to the Worldwatch Institute, sixteen of the twenty most polluted cities in the world are in China.[5]

Still, in the long term, it is in the developed nations' best interest to help developing countries adopt their own plans for sustainability, because only through this process can a solution be found to the problems of poverty, overpopulation, migration, and environmental decline. In this era of interdependency and shrinking distances, the developed and developing worlds are inextricably linked.

The process that began in Rio need not be frightening or antagonistic. It is an opportunity for people around the world to come together and work toward a livable future, both within their own nations and on the international level. Green Plans, with their promise of ideas, experiences, and knowledge to be shared among nations, provides just such an opportunity.

CHAPTER THREE

Health Plus Environment · Equals Security

One of the great policy successes of the late twentieth century was the recognition of the prevention of chronic and latent disease as a legitimate and important job for government. Another was the acceptance of the need for public initiatives to protect the environment for future generations. Both of these accomplishments depended on the premise that the future . . . is important. —*Frank Ackerman and Lisa Heinzerling*

One of the major factors drawing together communities, societies, and nations is, and has been throughout history, a common need for security. Thus, we could think of security as the basis of politics and a definer of history. Traditionally, security has been thought of mostly in military terms. Lately, we've begun to recognize that security is also closely entwined with environment. Recent examples include the devastating tidal wave that killed thousands in Asia or the effects of Hurricane Katrina on New Orleans.

A glance through history, with its rise and fall of civilizations, offers ample proof that the two are intimately related. Civilizations as advanced as the Maya, for example, in Central America, are thought to have died out because of a combination of environmental stress, which culminated in crop failure and disease, along with exhaustion from warfare and social decadence. In dry areas, irrigation, the means by which deserts can be made to bloom, can, over time, poison the soil and kill the crops needed for survival. Advanced civilizations, such as the Ancient Puebloans in the American Southwest, disappeared during the course of a period of prolonged drought. Another, more lush example is Easter Island, where in just a few centuries the islanders wiped out or devoured their forest, plants, and animals, denuding the sixty-four-square-acre island and reducing their complex society to poverty and cannibalism.[1]

Now, in our own time, when acid rain from the smokestacks of English factories can render lifeless entire systems of Scandinavian lakes, we can clearly see a direct link between environmental pollution and a threat to a major food source. When citizens can't eat fish, breathe air, or drink water without hurting their health, we can see that the environmental problem is becoming a problem of security in a very personal sense.

SECURITY THREATS: PERSONAL AND NATIONAL

Certain diseases have surfaced recently and become recognized as national security threats, which can affect tourism and travel, as in the case of Severe Acute Respiratory Syndrome (SARS), and whole economies and trade, as in the case of Mad Cow Disease (bovine spongiform encephalopathy). Thanks perhaps to an increasingly warming earth, diseases such as the mosquito borne West Nile Fever, are spreading from Africa all the way to the coast of California bringing with it, on currents of warmer than normal air, exotic disease and death. In some areas, now as in history, the carrying capacity of the land has collapsed. Populations have outgrown their land's ability to support them. Sudan is an example. Having consumed their forests, the various tribes struggled to meet their needs in the face of drought. In the ensuing civil war, tens of thousands have perished or been relocated.

So, to look beyond the immediate political problems, we can see that environmental mismanagement combined with economic and religious conflicts can lead to a collapse of security with catastrophic results. As amply recorded in the past, when environmental degradation threatens the health and happiness of populations, security breaks down. Health and environment, therefore, are crucial factors in personal and national security.

THE EXAMPLE OF MERCURY

Without presenting all of the myriad examples of the impact of environmental degradation on human health, I will look at just one example in detail, mercury, as it affected the people of Minimata, Japan, in the fifties. This story in its familiarity, prevalence, and gravity stands as one example of a polluting industry that is capable of devastating the health of a population, but then begins to accept responsibility. First, some general facts about mercury.

Mercury contamination is becoming a worldwide, frightening reality that affects industrialized areas and pristine wilderness alike. For example, in the vast expanses of the Arctic Circle, indigenous people are being poisoned by the high mercury levels found in the fish they catch and the animals they hunt for food. Because mercury is a byproduct of one of the most prevalent, and increasing, industrial processes—the burning of coal by power plants—and because mercury contamination poses such a direct and proven threat to human beings, it could arguably be called the worst of the common pollutants we have to deal with today.

What Exactly Is Mercury and How Does It Affect Us?

Mercury is found in nature in metallic, organic, or inorganic form. It is usually found in rocks and minerals such as cinnabar ore (HgS) and fossil fuels. On its own, undisturbed, it is not harmful. But when rocks are smashed, or coal is burned, mercury is released into the air, where it can waft over hundreds of miles, depositing itself on trees and land or streams, lakes, and oceans. That is when it becomes dangerous. In combination with biological elements, such as carbon, mercury becomes methylmercury, a deadly neurotoxin.

How Does Mercury Affect Our Health?

Methylmercury is a neurotoxin that, depending on the extent of exposure, can create systemic, irreversible damage to humans, and is particularly devastating to children and the unborn. In these vulnerable populations, damage can range from delayed development to mental retardation, neurological impairment, and even death.

Think of it as poison. In fact, mercury has actually been used as a poison of choice through much of history. Tasteless, colorless, and odorless it has been favored by assassins for its efficiency and ease of use. Less than a tenth of an ounce, and a human dies. The murder needn't be sudden. The poison accumulates in the body over time. So small amounts of mercury, added to the King's drink each evening, and, slowly, without causing suspicion, he falls ill and eventually lapses into a paralysis, stupor, and finally, death. Some have it that Napoleon was dispatched in this way.

In less dramatic form, similar poisoning is occurring all over the world every day. Here in America, 630,000 of the 4 million babies born each year are exposed to dangerous mercury levels in the womb.[2] What is the source of the mercury? Their own mothers, who have unknowingly eaten fish containing high mercury levels, thinking it was a healthy choice.

How Do Fish Get Contaminated by Mercury?

Mercury, as I've said, rises from smokestacks of coal-powered energy plants, and moves on the wind all over the globe, settling on land and water. Fish feeding on contaminated algae and also smaller fish take in the mercury, which then accumulates in their bodies. The health hazard for humans is that when they consume the larger fish, with their high concentrations of mercury, that mercury then begins to accumulate in their own bodies.

Mercury contamination is a global problem. Other than pollution from automobile exhaust, which, with the industrialization of China and India, continues to increase, most of the modern air pollution, including mercury contamination, comes from energy plants burning coal. The Environmental Protection Agency (EPA) notes that coal burned by electrical power plants in the United States accounts for one-third of all mercury pollution in the country. "Approximately 75 tons of mercury are found in the coal delivered to power plants each year and about two-thirds of this mercury is emitted to the air, resulting in about 50 tons being emitted annually."[3] Now, China too is burning increasing amounts of coal to feed its growing demand for energy. Again, emissions from these plants do not remain a local problem, but move on the wind around the world.

Pediatricians at Mount Sinai School of Medicine, in a 2005 study titled *Public Health and Economic Consequences of Methylmercury Toxicity to the Developing Brain*, calculated that damage to children's health from mercury poisoning costs the United States $8.7 billion each year.[4] This is a problem we cannot afford to ignore.

The cause, the prevalence, and the danger of mercury pollution illustrate the need for a broad management approach. As of 2005, the problem has long been known, yet the U.S. government places no limits on mercury emissions from power plants. Why? Attempts to put controls into affect have always been turned back by special interest lobbyists.

Fig. 2. Minamata, Japan. Relatives mourn loved ones lost to Minamata's Disease, caused by mercury poisoning. *Photo copyright Michael S. Yamashita/ CORBIS*

This is a good example of the negative effect on the health and economy of the nation that results from both the political process and the narrow focus of American industry, which funds these lobbying efforts. Ironically, the ultimate downside, should nothing be done, may befall industry itself. By limiting government's ability to put public health protections in place, these groups may themselves be found to be legally responsible and monetarily liable for public illness. The tobacco companies, we might recall, lost billions in law suits over the health consequences of their product and marketing tactics.

A good example, from the 1960s, of the cost to industries that ignore the health risks of their operations, is the occurrence of what became known as Minamata's Disease. This disease was named for the village in Japan in which the populace became sickened, crippled, or died over time, as part of the first documented large-scale incidence of mercury poisoning. At first a mystery, the source of the mercury was eventually traced to Minamata Bay. Its fish and shellfish, the village's primary food supply, were found to be highly contaminated with mercury. The source of the contamination was found to be a nearby plant, which produced acetaldehyde, a chemical used for a variety of things including perfumes, dyes, and solvents, among others. It is highly poisonous. The company at first claimed innocence, but eventually, under the pressure of the courts, complied; prison sentences were sought for retired executives, and the company is still paying medical care for some sufferers.[5]

I read of another example while waiting for an airplane in the Salt Lake City airport. There in the front page of the May 1, 2005, Sunday *Salt Lake Herald Tribune* was an in-depth article exposing the fact that mercury, a deadly poison, as I've said, is being carried into Utah on the wind, from the neighboring state of Nevada. The reporter, Patty Henetz, wrote that the mercury originates from a process being used by huge new gold mines. The article mentioned that the wind, which flows over neighboring states, carries enough mercury to represent 11 percent of total mercury emissions being released as a pollutant in the nation.[6]

In what is a classic situation these days, the government officials in charge seemed to know little about the issue. One was quoted as saying that they hadn't gotten around to measuring the mercury content of local fish, for instance, and that they were still doing scientific reviews, even though the measuring process—and the resulting mercury pollution—is quite common elsewhere.

EDUCATION IS CRUCIAL

Learning about a health threat from the point of view of environmental mismanagement will help the voting public move closer to understanding the need for—and to demand—a proper management approach.

Sustainability can't be left to government, or any particular administration, alone. Recently, federally elected officials have been trying to limit the requirement that coal-burning utilities use more effective (and expensive) controls to limit the release of mercury into our environment. Why would anyone try to evade health measures? In a system where campaign contributions are huge and must come from private sources, one will find that contributions—past or future—are in part behind the elected officials' attempts to look the other way when it comes to expensive health measures. This is a no-win process.

However, common sense and integrity can prevail, and in the case of the wind-borne mercury coming into Utah, the four largest companies are now voluntarily beginning to apply technology to stop the releases from the smokestacks. It is not enough, but it is a start.

WHAT CAN THE PUBLIC DO OR HOPE FOR?

Mercury, just to take one example, is so serious an economic and public health threat that it amounts to a disaster in the making. There is a simple answer to managing the problem. If, as was finally the case in Japan over mercury poisoning, the executives, corporations, or government agencies responsible for pollution were threatened with jail sentences or serious fines, you can be sure it would stop immediately. No executive is willing to spend a night in jail over a corporate problem.

AVOIDING THE LESSONS OF THE PAST

Somehow, despite the examples before us, we seem reluctant to apply the lessons learned from the past. Over the last several centuries we have acted toward our natural resources as if there were no limits and that we could take as much as we wanted and more would always be there. If scarcity were threatened, we seemed to expect that technological advances would be ready to solve the problems as they came up. I always remember a speech by President Eisenhower in which he said that soon we could stop worrying about having enough energy, because we would shortly have nuclear sources and unlimited energy supplies. Now while we have continued to expand our need for energy, we have learned that nuclear energy is not the solution. While the daily operating emissions from nuclear plants shouldn't pollute the air, accidents—such as happened at Chernoble—that release radioactive fumes are hell itself. Nuclear power comes with significant problems, and so the world is scrambling uneasily to find more supplies of fossil fuels.

In 1987, the United Nations established a commission to study and define the problem. As part of its study, the Brundtland Commission visited many of the world's problem sites. Among its conclusions was the idea that we could and must manage not just part but all of our environmental problems if we are to avert large-scale environmental collapse. The commission realized that, given the interconnected nature of the ecosystem and the global nature of our relationships, we can't solve only *some* of the environmental problems; we must work to solve *all* of the environmental problems.

Lest this sound impossible, the commission invented a management approach to stretch the availability of natural resources. They named it sustainable management, which I've discussed at length in this book. Implicit in all of its recommendations is the awareness that a healthy environment is both good for its own sake, necessary for the health of individuals, and essential for the security of nations. While this awareness and management approach is a huge step in the right direction, there are still vast chasms to be crossed before human beings achieve the dream of security.

WHAT IS NECESSARY TO REALIZE THE DREAM OF SECURITY?

One next step could be to review the current problems facing us and to realize that the health of the environment is a not an option, to be considered at leisure after all economic goals are met, but a practical, essential requirement for any society and the world at large.

When we recognize environmental health as a requirement, we can see that we are falling short. The symptoms are right in front of us. We're experiencing shortages of materials. We're suffering health problems. Developed nations are consuming resources at an unsustainable rate, while developing nations suffer famines and wars stemming from environmental collapse. In our own country, we have suffered such a threat to our security that it has rearranged all of our priorities, favoring military and economic goals over all else. And the environment is suffering. We need a serious commitment to a comprehensive plan to assure the health of our environment and our children well into the future.

LIMITS, SHORTAGES, AND THE REQUIREMENTS OF MAINTAINING SECURITY

Despite the evidence in front of us, here in the United States, we tend to resist the notion of limits even while we encounter shortages of what once seemed to be a limitless supply. New conditions call for rethinking and behavior adjustment by government and citizens. Take an example from our own colonial history.

In the seventeenth and eighteenth centuries, England, the world's foremost sea power, had a vast appetite for tall straight trees, which they converted into the masts of ships. But being a small country, the English were starting to run short. The trees simply couldn't grow as fast as they were needed for the constant demand for new ships. And having new ships was necessary for trade and defense, for that, for the English, at that time, meant security. Because other European powers at the time also required trees for shipbuilding, the shortage of usable trees for masts was dire.

So England had to go to other places to get their straight tall trees. One of these was the area around Boston, New Hampshire, and New York. English soldiers combed the countryside looking for the highly desirable trees. And when they found one, they branded it with the king's royal symbol. They didn't pay for it; instead soldiers came along and cut down the tree and shipped it back to England. The king viewed taking the trees for free as his right. As one might expect, American landowners whose trees were removed were angry at the practice. It was one of the agitating factors that caused the American Revolution.

A similar story is currently being played out with oil. As developing nations begin to industrialize, they need oil and gas for their new cars. So they begin to share not only the high costs of fuel shortages, but the health and environmental problems brought on by air pollution. The current levels of air pollution in China and India, for example, are practically paralyzing.[7] The dreams of economists, that consumption and growth can only be a good thing, are about to hit a wall. Like the security threat caused by the lack of trees for the tall ships' masts, today's economy, based on ever-increasing consumption, is precariously balanced on its dependence on a finite supply of fossil fuel, the ill-health the burning of it currently promotes, and the knowledge that supplies are running short.

LIMITLESS CONSUMPTION: A WORLD OUT OF BALANCE

The ever-increasing rate of consumption of the world's resources is resulting in both increasing amounts of waste and shortages of resources. Together these conditions represent disaster for the environment and a threat to personal and national security. Even now, current wars, such as the civil war in the Sudan, as I have mentioned, can be traced to problems resulting from environmental collapse. Whereas in sixteenth-century England the threat was dealt with by building more ships for defense, in our modern world we're obsessed with solving the world's problems through oil exploration and economic trade.

As we can see by the evidence all around us—by the growing scarcity of resources previously considered limitless, by the increasing health problems among our citizens, by the threat of new and exotic diseases—environmental health is on the decline. And with that, so is our security, both national and personal. Basing our policies on the purely economic model has not worked. A significant move toward overall health and security would be to begin to manage the environment and the economy realistically. To do that, we have to first recognize the relationships.

CONNECTING THE DOTS

Environment is not just trees and water and picturesque landscapes that we may view as a sort of optional ideal. Environment is essential to the existence of humanity. We are part of it. It is part of us. It's not possible to have a healthy individual, whether plant, animal, or human, in an unhealthy environment. Epidemics of asthma in southern California are directly associated with toxins from auto exhaust polluting the air. Malaria is moving north, a result of global warming. Here and in Europe, whole forests are dying because of emissions from distant factories and industrial centers borne on acid rain.

In terms of personal health and security, scientists currently worry about the growing threat of wide-scale epidemics of diseases for which we have no cure. Bird flu, for example, is a swiftly mutating disease for which a vaccine has only just been discovered. The dire forecasts of a pandemic like the deadly influenza of 1918 that killed between twenty and forty million people—more than died in World War I—did not become reality in *this* case. Industrial livestock production relies on concentrating tens of thousands of animals, which increases the likelihood of disease transfer and creates myriad environmental challenges. While economics dictate factory farm conditions like those that lead to bird flu and other widespread animal viruses, zoonotic disease—that which spreads between people and animals—is already a reality and enduring threat.

HEALTH AND SECURITY PUT THE STEAM IN THE ENGINE OF PLANNING

What does all this have to do with Green Plans? The examples in this chapter show that environmental health impacts personal health and that both impact personal and global security. All over the world, the need is urgent, therefore, for comprehensive planning in the interests of environmental health. The Green Plan countries, in which stakeholders work together to solve the entire environmental problem through comprehensive resource management, are successfully moving toward sustainability, a necessary condition for health and security.

CHAPTER FOUR

A Green Plan Predecessor

California's Investing for
Prosperity Program

The need for a comprehensive, integrated form of resource management became clear to me during my experiences in government. There I saw firsthand the sorts of problems that can arise when we attempt to manage the environment in the traditional way, dealing with single-purpose issues one at a time. This was particularly obvious when confronted by a sudden, massive, complex environmental challenge such as a drought, which forces cities to compete with agriculture for water and sets the stage for huge wildfires that burn for miles and consume homes and vegetation, which in turn clears the way for floods and mudslides.

From 1977 to 1982, I was head of the California Resources Agency. This is the state-level version of a minister of environment. The department's budget at that time was nearly $1 billion and it had fourteen thousand employees. As a member of the cabinet of Governor Edmund G. (Jerry) Brown Jr., I was responsible for the administration's resource policies, including overseeing policy and budgets on water, forests, wildlife, energy, and others. Many challenges we faced at that time, and the solutions we devised, are still applicable to our current crisis.

First of all, California is heavily resource-dependent. Tourism, agriculture, and timber production are three of its largest industries, and its fisheries have traditionally been important as well, although they have suffered badly in recent years as wild fish populations have declined. In addition, California is a heavy consumer of energy and water for agricultural, industrial, and residential uses. When I took the job, my goal was to promote the idea of stewardship of resources as a public trust. I felt that, in California and the nation as a whole, we had thought only of harvesting and consuming the cornucopia of our natural resources. We had failed to understand, or had chosen to ignore, the fact that these natural systems require sensitive management to keep them healthy. I did not set out to develop a comprehensive, integrated plan for dealing with California's resources; I realized the importance of such a plan only when forced to confront the pressures that the energy crisis of the 1970s put on the state and its resources. Energy was a relatively new issue in those days, although it had been brought home with great force by the Arab oil embargo of the early 1970s, when the price of oil went up more than 150 percent and sent energy prices through the roof. That increase was a threat to the state's entire economy, and the Resources Agency naturally spent a great deal of time reacting to the fallout from the crisis.[1]

A great many people believed that they had the answer to the problem, and the advocates of nuclear power were some of the loudest among them. I was against relying on the development of nuclear power, primarily because there are no reasonable solutions for dealing with the waste. One of the things I did when I first took office, then, was to oppose plans for more nuclear plants. With the governor's support, the Resources Agency announced that it was going to oppose all new nuclear power plants.

California was already facing a serious threat to the economy from the energy crisis, so that decision caused a tremendous public-relations furor. The utilities fired back that they had to have an energy growth rate of 7 percent per year forever, and that California would shiver in the dark if its nuclear power generation were not increased. Some years later, the then-president of the largest utility, not just in California, but also in the world, publicly thanked us for taking a stand against the industry's plans to build forty nuclear plants up and down the state. If his utility had carried out its plans, he later said, the ultimate cost would have driven them bankrupt.

IN SEARCH OF A COMPREHENSIVE SOLUTION

But stopping nuclear power development still left us with the problems caused by the energy crisis. As the angry calls poured into the agency, asking what we were going to do about it, we struggled to come up with an answer, to devise an energy policy that would make sense for the future. One night I literally awoke to the realization that this issue affected every other issue my department dealt with.

For instance, a portion of the state's air quality problems come from the process of burning oil in order to create the energy to pump the water. This led to the realization that the poor air quality was somehow affecting trees and crops; we did not understand how or why, but our suspicions were later confirmed when the problems of acid rain were better understood.

All that is to say that the interactions of humans and their environment need to be dealt with in a comprehensive way, because they reach further than one initially realizes, and are all interconnected. Faced with the far-reaching crisis in energy, that understanding struck me with great force. At that point I began to develop plans for a more comprehensive resource strategy, which came to be called Investing for Prosperity (IFP).

The philosophy behind the IFP was this: Nature has its own time scale. It takes one hundred years to make an inch of productive topsoil, a half-century to produce commercial timber, and decades to restore degraded rangeland. If we tie our response to the erosion of our resources to annual government budgets, fought over from year to year and from crisis to crisis, we will never succeed. Until we have a comprehensive and integrated plan, we cannot move forward.

California had many resource problems, even beyond the immediate ones caused by the energy crisis, which called out for such a comprehensive plan. The state's timber production had been declining for two decades, to the point where commercial timberlands were producing less than 50 percent of their capacity. Salmon runs were dropping precipitously, and the productivity of thousands of acres of farmland was threatened by erosion, increasing soil salinity, and the results of air pollution.[2]

The idea behind the IFP was to establish funding for and set up programs to restore and improve many aspects of the state's natural resources. The Resources Agency was able to show that the returns to the state would be well worth the investment. Eventually we got a series of laws passed that provided more than $120 million a year (which would be much more than that today) for investment in long-term quality and productivity programs for California's natural resources.

The relevant fact for this book and for the Green Plan idea is that these programs have now been in existence for twenty-five years. Where other comprehensive strategies are too new to assess with much accuracy, this one has measurable results. More than a billion dollars has been invested in IFP programs, and they have returned billions on the investment. Taking a close look at them is one way to evaluate the potential success of the Green Plan idea.

Some of the programs that the energy fund invested in were

government efforts, since we believed we had to show the way before we could expect the rest of society to follow. These projects included streetlight retrofits, replacing old light bulbs with more energy-efficient ones; conservation in schools and hospitals; insulation of hot-water pipes, and more efficient motors placed in machines of all types as part of new appliance and building standards. The retrofit program for streetlights alone is now saving cities some $2 million per year, while the $45.3 million that the IFP loaned to schools and hospitals to develop cogeneration projects (systems that use heat energy that would otherwise be wasted) continues to produce savings.

At that time, we invested $48 million in energy conservation and alternative sources. By 1988, energy use at state facilities had been cut by 20 percent; our goal was a 40 percent cut by the year 2000. Our goal for energy development of alternative sources such as cogeneration, geothermal, solar, and biomass was 400 megawatts; by 1990 we had achieved 191. By 1990, the combined savings to the state from these energy programs was about $333 million.[3] Despite the fact that we did not reach our initial goals, the savings we achieved were quite substantial. In addition, our efforts inspired industry to make a massive turn toward conservation, and businesses soon took the lead on energy efficiency. The success of the program rested on the comprehensive cooperation of government agencies responding to my appeal.

There were many individuals and departments that helped make this investment in energy alternatives a reality, such as the California State Energy Commission and the Office for Appropriate Technology, as well as a legion of committed individuals. The California legislature, which responded to the challenge of the energy issue early on, was also a major player.

The success of the energy component of the IFP was also due to the support of individuals and organizations outside of government. Examples include the corporate leaders who adopted the idea and ran with it, the managers of institutions such as hospitals and schools who did the same, and everybody right on down to the people who turned off the lights in their closets. These were the people who started an energy revolution in California.

Unfortunately, we have not followed through with the same enthusiasm on other issues, including water, soil, wildlife, and air. But there have been changes in these areas, too—and there will be more over time—that may one day look just as good as our successes in energy conservation. At least better policies are in place for air quality, and they are starting to fall into place for water.

THE FIGHT FOR PASSAGE

Because time was of the essence in getting the IFP legislation passed, the Resources Agency did not conduct public hearings or field hearings. That would have been the ideal in terms of building a strong constituency for the programs, and it is what New Zealand did for its Resource Management Act. But the conditions we faced were difficult. Our decision to stop nuclear development was already creating an uproar of a dimension I could not have imagined. Attacks came at us from all sides, orchestrated by the public relations firms hired by the utilities.

Worse, the state was in the throes of its taxpayer rebellion, which would eventually lead to Proposition 13 and its severe curtailment of government revenues from property taxes. The order went out that there would be no new programs; government spending had to be cut. I believed that, instead of being a negative, the Proposition 13 crisis had to be the catalyst for a new attitude toward resource management. The environment had to be seen as an investment, not just another expense, because ultimately it is these resources upon which the economy and our quality of life are based. But I knew that it would take quick and aggressive action to win my point.

Fortunately, I was able to move aggressively because I had trusted allies, the people I had brought in to head the various departments under me: Forestry, Fish and Game, Water, and so on. I asked them to find the dreamers in their departments—those who were the brightest and most able, but also the most frustrated—and pull together all their ideas for improving the departments' effectiveness.

Once they had done this we had several meetings to discuss the results, and within a few weeks I was able to lay out what would become the Investing for Prosperity fund. I then had to go and sell it statewide and proceeded to do so with the help of those departments, which now had a stake in the issue.

We signed on constituency groups like the League of Women Voters, which adopted the resource fund idea as its statewide project for the year. One useful political lesson we learned was that politicians respected the League. It had eighty chapters throughout the state. No politician wanted to have a phone call from a respected local chapter of informed citizens, critical of that politician's approach.

The Audubon Society was the first environmental group to support the IFP, followed by all the others. Eventually, even the labor unions and corporations, including heavyweights like IBM, Southern Pacific Railroad, and the Bank of America, came to understand what we were doing and openly supported us.

One example of how we were able to forge such a strong coalition is the approach we took to the forest industry. I went directly to the main lobbying organization for the entire forest industry, which would typically have opposed the agency on this issue. I met with the director and laid out the plan, and he said he would check with his constituents and get back to me. When he did, he said, "I'll surprise you: They're willing to cooperate, but they have one requirement."

That requirement turned out to be an interesting challenge. The forestry industry's concern was that about one-third of

California's timberland was not producing. One reason was that the small, private owners and investors could not afford to replant their land and then wait fifty years for a new crop of trees. If I could figure out something that would help the small owners to get trees in the ground and make their lands productive, then the forest industry would help me on the big picture. That included lobbying in the areas of energy efficiency, water, and whatever else it would take to pass this bill for $125 million a year in resource investment.

So the agency created a grant program for small timber owners. In order to get a grant, though, the owners had to put together a productivity plan, prepared by a professional forester, which would lay out the long-term future for the lands involved. They could then apply for a grant to do whatever needed to be done, whether it was building bridges, improving their roads, planting trees, or preparing forests.

Jeff Romm of the University of California's Department of Forestry has since said that the most important part of this program was its requirement of stewardship; that the owners had to put together a management plan for the future.[4] It changed their attitude and outlook, he said, so that henceforth in their meetings, individually, or in the professional associations, they would talk about the long term; they would no longer just talk about getting board feet off the land. Although the program started out primarily as a push to get trees planted, the philosophical point has proved more powerful.

The lesson to learn from the timber growers is that everyone has something to gain from improving the quality and productivity of the environment. This appeal to a wide variety of interests is one of the strengths of a comprehensive program. Some interests will be opposed to parts of it, but because many more will benefit from it as a whole, the opposition will find it harder to block. Any state that goes through a Green Plan process will have to reach out to all the individual interest groups and build a powerful constituency for change.

Between 1978 and 1980, with coalition building and other hard work, the Resources Agency was able to achieve passage of all five pieces of legislation that created the legal and financial basis for the IFP. Taken together, they constituted a program of investment in California's natural resources that aimed to put the state back on healthy environmental and economic ground within twenty years, while looking ahead one hundred years to the legacy we would leave our grandchildren. Because of their success, many of the IFP's programs continue to be funded, despite several changes in state government since then.

Five laws established the IFP:

- The Forest Improvement Act, which provided for an urban forestry program and cost-sharing of reforestation on small, private tree-farm forest lands
- The Forest Resources Development Fund, which established the principle that income from the sale of state-owned timber would be reinvested to improve forest productivity and implement urban tree-planting programs
- The Renewable Resources Investment Fund, which provided $10 million to develop wood energy, help restore salmon stocks, and implement water conservation and reclamation projects
- The Geothermal Resources Fund, which provided that 30 percent of the income from federal geothermal leases in California be deposited in the Renewable Resources Investment Fund
- The Energy and Resources Fund, which allocated a portion of the state's tidelands oil revenues for the restoration and protection of the state's renewable resources[5]

Under the program, the funds made available by the legislation were to be invested in a number of resource areas. Specific goals were established for each and projects implemented to achieve them. The main areas were forestry and wildlands, fish and wildlife, water, soils, coastal resources, parks and recreation, and energy.

In response to the energy crisis, we had the following goals for the year 2000: to reduce by 40 percent the amount of energy used by state government operations, to continue to expand and encourage efficiency, to develop efficient and renewable energy production technologies, and to reduce gasoline consumption by 40 percent of the 1980 levels.[6] We decided early on that there was no one black box, like nuclear power, that was going to be the answer to our energy problems. Instead we used what I called a principle of portions. We learned that any small amount of alternative energy you could produce, even as little as a half of a percent, would in time accumulate, together with the savings from conservation and the energy created by other alternative sources, into a big block of energy that could fulfill the state's needs. There was considerable pioneering in the development of alternatives to fossil fuels in those years, such as cogeneration, biomass, solar, and geothermal.

Other programs have also done very well. From 1979 to 1988, $30 million was invested in salmon and steelhead restoration programs, 90 percent on the North Coast and 10 percent in the Central Valley. Five hundred and twenty-three restoration contracts were funded, about half of what we had originally hoped to fund. However, we surpassed our original goal of clearing the blockages from five hundred miles of streams so that salmon could swim up into them and spawn freely; by 1988, fourteen hundred miles had been cleared.[7]

Back then it was difficult to assess the impact of a program like the salmon and steelhead restoration in the short term, because other factors cause fluctuations in the results. In this instance there was one huge blip upward, after which the fisheries again began to decline. Much of this has been blamed on high-seas netting, in which Korean, Taiwanese, and Japanese fishermen were creating walls of drift nets out in the ocean that trapped anything that swam, including salmon and steelhead. This has now been largely changed through international treaties.

In the forestry sector, part of the plan was to help reforest a million acres with 360 million trees, to reverse the decline in timber productivity. A study funded by a subsequent governor's administration projected that, over the next fifty to seventy-five years, the $5 million spent on this project will return $448 million in timber sales, $104 million in tax revenues, and $9 million in consumer savings, while creating eighteen thousand new jobs.[8]

The IFP also had a goal of increasing the annual timber supply over 1980 levels by three billion board feet, through improved wood products utilization, integrated pest control, and forest and tree improvement efforts. That demonstrates the program's comprehensive approach: Instead of investment in just one thing, growing trees, it promoted such innovations as using thinner saw blades in the mills because they caused less waste than the old ones. It is the same principle of conservation that worked so well with energy.

The IFP proposed some changes in agriculture that were designed to conserve soil, particularly in terms of research into reducing the consumption of fuel and other oil by-products. Other ideas included minimum tillage, windbreaks, and integrated pest management—whatever one could do to cut down on the use of chemicals and tractors.

The IFP improved the state's urban resources, too. Substantial funding went to park development, beach erosion control, and reestablishing beaches in cities where they had been lost. It was this that convinced the labor movement to come along with the IFP. Labor unions understood the energy issue, but were not terribly excited about it. However, the idea of enhancing the quality of life for workers by investing in outdoor recreational opportunities did appeal to them. They liked the fact that we emphasized trail development, campground development, and other themes in the parks and recreation area.

Because water is such a scarce and precious resource in California, we also devoted a great deal of attention to water conservation projects for both agricultural and urban users. These projects included investing four million dollars in developing a computerized system for agricultural irrigation that was based on actual crop needs rather than farmers' traditional methods. Now twenty-five years later, the program is still working and has continued to be improved. Urban water conservation practices were encouraged by the distribution of more than four million kits to households throughout the state. This program saved 38,700 acre-feet of water and 940 million kilowatts of energy per year.[9] Subsequent conservation programs cut urban water use by one-sixth in a short period of time.

CHANGING GOVERNMENT

In the process of getting the IFP passed and implemented, I learned many valuable lessons about what it takes to make such a major change in government. One such lesson was how to get a program funded when it seemed impossible.

In spite of California's taxpayer revolt, we were successful in obtaining funding for this idea because we wove all the elements together into one big picture, in a way that reached industries and labor unions and environmental groups and educators and scientists. They supported it because they could see the vision behind it, and because all felt that they had a part in it.

On a pragmatic level, the experience also taught me how important it was to get all the relevant government agencies working together. For instance, on my first day on the job I found that the Energy Commission, whose budget I was responsible for, was suing the Forestry Department, another of the agencies under my authority, because of a conflict over water and energy issues. Neither of the two agencies had bothered to contact my predecessor.

When government agencies and policies are not integrated

in a comprehensive way, it leads to this kind of wasteful squabbling and creates tremendous inefficiencies. When the public sees this going on it loses faith in government, as was happening in this case. We could never have accomplished what we did if we had allowed that situation to continue.

The most important factor in the IFP's success is that we made it our top priority, and the governor was also committed to the idea. Leadership from the executive and managerial branches can be crucial through the inevitable political ups and downs. A program like this can only be maintained if it has been firmly planted.

Looking back for further lessons, I see that it was helpful having a central administrative focal point, which functions like an orchestra conductor, so that priorities could be established and adjusted. The next administration tried its best to kill what we had started. The new governor did not think much of our ideas; I believe he asserted that there is "no such thing as limits" in regard to resources. The energy crisis dissipated, and the new governor saw his role solely as one of creating jobs through growth. But those people who were committed to the program and stayed on in government were able to sustain it at about 80 percent of its original levels. The sound energy policy laid out by the IFP is fairly standard practice now, regardless of who is in office. Other individuals who believed strongly enough in the idea have kept it alive elsewhere.

The program and its goals caused a tremendous uproar, played out in the California legislature between the environmental movement and the utilities and other industries. But once the smoke had cleared, we had achieved something that benefited the whole state. It took a large and diverse coalition to accomplish it, but that coalition became one of its greatest strengths.

PART II

Assessing Green
Plans in Action

CHAPTER FIVE

The Netherlands

In Amsterdam's Rijksmuseum, known for its collection of paintings by the Dutch masters, there is one painting that looms above all the rest. It is by Rembrandt, and it forever changed the world's ideas about art. It is titled *The Night Watch*, and it looks as though it were painted in three dimensions. When you look at it, the hand appears to be reaching out to you. Rembrandt startled the world with that painting, so much so that it changed our ideas of art forever. I believe the Netherlands' National Environmental Policy Plan (NEPP) will similarly change the way people see themselves and their actions in relation to the environment. I care so much about finding an answer to environmental decline, that I also believe the individuals who have come together to form this Dutch Plan should be remembered as having created a work at least as important as Rembrandt's. When I look today at the continued emergence of the comprehensive view, which the Dutch have handled so well, I believe it's starting to have a universal appeal.

When an idea is important enough, it can overcome opposi-

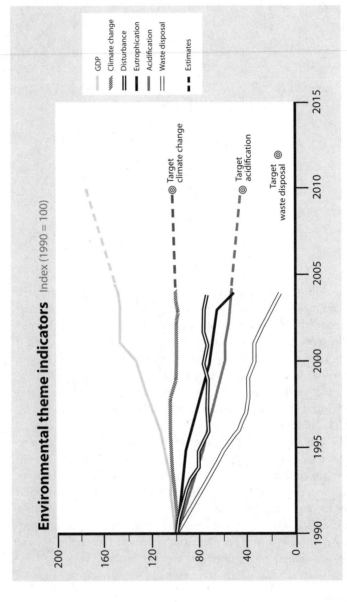

Environmental theme indicators Index (1990 = 100)

Legend:
- GDP
- Climate change
- Disturbance
- Eutrophication
- Acidification
- Waste disposal
- Estimates

Target climate change

Target acidification

Target waste disposal

200
160
120
80
40
0

1990 1995 2000 2005 2010 2015

Fig. 3. Environmental theme indicators, 1990

tion and obstacles and survive. The Dutch National Environmental Policy Plan is an example of that principle and serves as a guiding framework for creating real improvement of the environment.

Since its introduction in 1989, the Dutch Plan has continued, as it was structured, to guide the Netherlands toward its agreed-upon goal of environmental recovery in twenty-five years. That the Plan continues despite swings in the economy and changes in political parties, and even though results are not perfect, is a remarkable achievement. Other similar endeavors, such as many that began in the United States, have faltered and died en route; yet the Dutch, as a society, still hold onto the dream and share the common objective of total environmental recovery at every level. It is so accepted and unquestioned in its central approach that it has become part of their value system and standard behavior. The Dutch know it will only succeed if everyone participates, so they've made it a "social contract." A crucial part of their planning process has been the participation and involvement of all stakeholders.

YOU CAN ONLY SOLVE ALL OF THE PROBLEM

The strength of the NEPP is that it is comprehensive and yet flexible enough to respond to new challenges. All the participants, including all of the institutions and corporations in the country, are bound by the common purpose of total restoration of environmental health within twenty-five years. Specific time-bound long-term targets give everyone a clear and stable compass for this long-term endeavor. This allows solutions to be tied in with business investment cycles and makes everyone's share accountable and transparent.

The comprehensive nature of the Dutch Plan is the result of careful thought by hundreds of the country's brightest people who have managed for the first time ever to put a nation's complex, interrelated natural systems into a manageable context.

The NEPP successfully weaves together complex systems such as water, air, soil, and energy, and meshes them with human factors, economics, health, and carrying capacity. It is a comprehensive, long-term, well-thought-out plan, and the Dutch have committed billions of guilders into implementing it.

Whereas traditional environmental programs have tended not to work well in the real world because they focused on one or two problems and were not involved with overall management, this strong, comprehensive management framework has helped make the Dutch Plan practical and functional. When it comes to the environment, you can only solve *all* of the problem, taking into account all the interrelationships. The name "Green Plan" means that the whole spectrum of environmental issues is managed together to avoid partial solutions and to foster synergy. The problem is made operational and manageable by defining quantitative medium- and short-term emission targets and specifying the contribution of each sector of the economy.

A THOUSAND SHADES OF GREEN

Emphasis on good management has led the Dutch to some interesting innovations, particularly in the way they deal with industry. For example, they encourage each industrial sector to pledge to deliver its fair share toward meeting the agreed-upon long-term targets. It also allows them to work out for themselves, in cooperation with the government, their plans for achieving the required, measurable emission-reduction goals. While everyone is bound by the long-term goal, individual institutions can create their own strategies within the comprehensive plan.

Industry seems to like the Green Plan idea because it gives them long-term stable targets to include in their plans and budget. It also gives them flexibility, whereas the traditional, old style of regulation from the top down, overseen and enforced by some government agency, is slower to react to needed changes. In the old style, individual industries may be confronted by sudden demands for immediate changes, which result in greater cost and a great deal more conflict between factions in society because they lack a cooperative, agreed-upon goal and direction.

In the Dutch system, corporations have the discretion to plan and budget their changes on their own schedule, as long as over-all choices ensure the realization of the agreed-upon goals. In other words, the Dutch Plan focuses more on the goals than the means; and with a proper, certified, environmental care system underpinning these efforts, they increase efficiency and reduce bureaucratic red tape. That freedom of choice, and freedom to plan and budget, is a great advantage to a company. Depending on what they manufacture or produce, companies can select those portions that are going to affect their particular operations. Without it being said, the foreboding reality is that if they don't comply on a cooperative basis, the Netherlands government will revert to the old command-and-control regime and they will be forced to comply, with possibly untimely, costly, and disruptive orders from above.

Pieter Winsemius is a physicist and management specialist who was minister of the environment during the NEPP planning phase. He refers to this flexibility as "a thousand shades of green."[1] The ways in which companies respond to environmental challenges can be as different as the companies themselves.

Time has proven this concept right. After eighteen years, Dutch industry—Royal Shell Oil, Royal Philips Electric, Unilever, and others—carry on with environmental quality management, often in ways that are better than the government requires. Good environmental practice, enforced by periodic review from the National Institute for Public Health and the Environment, not to mention the ever-present watchdog of public opinion, has become a habit for corporations and individuals as well.

Another aspect of the genius of the Dutch Plan is the twenty-five-year time frame they have set for achieving environmental recovery. Their slogan, "Each generation cleans up," reminds them that the twenty-five years, or one generation, is a common goal that every citizen can support. It clearly echoes the Brundt-land definition of sustainability, that is, not to fulfill their needs by undermining options for future generations.

This twenty-five-year time frame is key to providing business and industry the flexibility to approach the goal in a way that works for them, but within the context of the whole. Each year they have to announce their plans for the coming year. Will they focus on water this next year, or air quality, conserve more energy, or buy more machinery? Whatever it might be, they make a decision and at the end of the year turn in their accomplishments. They are judged by how successful they've been in meeting the goals they've set out for themselves, but still have to be seriously working on the total package until the goal is reached. So they have flexibility, but it's clearly not "anything goes." The "voluntary agreements" in which the negotiated contribution of industry is captured sometimes easily give rise to the latter impression; but it *is* an agreement and it is binding.

So far, the long-term approach is working. The original NEPP laid out the overall goals and objectives based on the assessment of the carrying capacity of ecosystems and human health. Long-term, measurable emission-reduction targets were established for environmental themes that covered the whole range of environmental problems.

For each sector of industry, their contribution to these targets was defined in close consultation. The original NEPP called for a series of four-year plans. These four-year plans contain reflections on what has been accomplished and what is needed for the next four years. It allows for adjustments in operations, but is basically a renewal for another four years of the NEPP. With each past renewal, the government could have elected not to continue, but each time, they have persisted. Although the new conservative government's emphasis is on security and the economy, and it hasn't expanded or advanced the Green Plan, it has maintained its ambition and kept it going. In fact, that very same government has announced that it will produce a strategic environmental policy agenda to keep up the momentum for environmental policy.

Currently, consultations are held with stakeholders, critics, and scientists to gather input for the next agenda. To date Holland has achieved well over half the legal and regulatory goals of the original objectives, and the required four-year plans themselves have been stated and carried out.

Closely related to the cycle of producing National Environmental Policy Plans is a policy document they produced in 1997 on environment and the economy. This document tried to capture the positive benefits of eco-efficient innovations for economic goals, such as growth and employment, and for emission-reduction goals involving energy and natural resource use.

The idea of achieving environmental goals by fostering the synergy between environmental protection and economic development was at the very heart of the Dutch presidency of the EU at the end of 2004. The general mood in Europe, around crucial dossiers like the Kyoto Protocol, was very much one of downplaying or delaying environmental ambition because of perceived impacts on global competition. Yet the Dutch launched what they call the "Clean, Clever, Competitive" approach[2] in which they underlined the positive advantages for jobs, growth, and competition from applying eco-innovations, or doing more with less. This approach was well received and recognized by heads of state as part of Europe's leading strategy to become the most innovative economy in the world.

WHY DOES THE NETHERLANDS' EFFORT WORK?

The Netherlands has a long tradition as one of the world's most progressive nations. It has maintained literacy at some of the highest levels in the world, and its different interests are well organized. It has always been in the forefront with its policies on quality-of-life issues such as health care. In creating and implementing the NEPP, the Dutch took the lead, and throughout eighteen years of steady application have shown the world that it is possible to solve the environmental problems that are of great concern to every nation. It has been able to maintain overall progress by adjusting and refocusing the plans as needed, given problems encountered in the implementation and within the broad framework.

All in all, solving these problems has seemed possible at affordable costs. Strong dialogue with the business sector has ensured that despite differences of opinion on certain issues, the support by industry for environmental policy has been high throughout the years. The "promise" of the Dutch government to pursue similar environmental demands within the European Union, thus safeguarding the competitive position of Dutch industry, helped to maintain industry support. For that reason, they have been active in establishing the carbon dioxide emission trading regime in Europe, and have come up with remarkable incentives for industry.[3] Also, as part of their policy document on environment and economy, the Dutch government signed a benchmark agreement with industry in which industry pledged to help the Netherlands be among the most energy efficient countries of the world. Living up to that promise, industry would be rewarded by the government not imposing any new additional national measures on energy saving.

There are many reasons why the Netherlands became the first nation to adopt and pursue a comprehensive national environmental strategy. A small, densely populated nation, the Netherlands is situated at the mouth of the Rhine, which in the mid-1980s was one of Europe's most polluted rivers. Every year the river deposited enormous quantities of contaminated silt at its mouth near Rotterdam. Almost half of the acid deposition in the Netherlands originated in other countries, particularly the surrounding nations of Germany, France, and Belgium, adding to the pollution contributed by the nation's own industries.

The Dutch have always been traders, and their economy lacks the natural resources of other countries such as the United States and Canada. They are heavily dependent on export-oriented, pollution-based industries such as commodity chemicals and metals, as well as industrialized agriculture, all contributing heavily to just about every environmental problem.

As of 2005, the Netherlands, a land about twice the size of New Jersey, supported a population numbering some 16,292,000 people.[4] This is about 245 people per square mile, compared to 79.6 people per square mile in the United States. If you add to that nearly 11 million pigs, over a million sheep, nearly 3.8 million cows, plus some 86 million poultry[5]—not to mention nearly 9 million automobiles—you can begin to imagine the enormous amount of pressure put on a small and environmentally vulnerable land, and why a comprehensive environmental plan would be necessary for a healthy quality of life.[6]

Another reason the Dutch became leaders in the field of environmental planning is that planning is not only familiar to them but something they welcome. Their huge system of dikes, windmills, and water *quantity* management has always been close to the country's heart. They have reclaimed enormous amounts of land from the sea in a period of about three centuries, and the process continues. The Netherlands as we know it simply would not exist without a great deal of intricate planning. Nevertheless, its vulnerability to the sea remains real. The Dutch are well aware that global warming, with its accompanying rising sea levels, could inundate them.

Finally, the Dutch are survivors. They have managed to remain economically successful for centuries even though they have very few natural resources. While other countries, like the United States and Canada, had huge forests and other resources they could exploit for an easy economic base, the Dutch had to learn to be careful, skilled traders and planners in order to survive. Most of their natural landscapes are "man-made." As a nation, they value cooperation and consensus in the realm of public affairs. They see defining national economic and social policy as a joint endeavor of government, trade unions, and business representatives. For all these reasons, Green Plans, a long-term comprehensive endeavor, founded in cooperation and consensus, forms an ideal structure for the Dutch. The fact that they have been so successful gives hope to others for the future. It demonstrates that results can be achieved and cooperation is possible without either side—government or industry—surrendering their responsibility or independence. Government can apply rules and industry can still oppose them.

HOW DOES THE NETHERLANDS MONITOR THEIR GREEN PLAN RESULTS?

In the Netherlands, progress toward the environmental goal is monitored by the National Institute for Public Health and the Environment (RIVM), an independent group of scientists who publish regular reports, accessible to all, on the Internet.[7] These reports operate much like an audit—the purpose is not to catch cheaters necessarily, but to make sure that everyone carries on in an honorable way. As an independent, institutionalized critic, whose integrity is beyond question, RIVM scientists look at the results each year and document all issues. In the Netherlands science remains pure and independent, unlike in the United States, where corporate executives can, as much for social reward as any depth of conviction, head up boards of the very environmental groups who should be watchdogging their corporations. The reputation of the RIVM is impeccable; people trust that if there are problems, the RIVM will let them know, and the alarm will go off. Government and industry respect the RIVM as well. What they do is keep everybody honest and make their assessments of progress, or the lack thereof, clear to everyone. Just like reporting on the national budget, they produce an annual *Environmental Balance* to keep track of the diminishment or increase of the "environmental debt."

Also critical to maintaining the momentum of the Plan and helping everyone move toward the shared goal are numerous groups who comprise the environmental movement. They're the watchdogs, snarling outside the meeting-room door where government and industry are negotiating policy. They have considerable power and if they issue a press release, or an accusation, it gets in the paper; the public pays attention.

All the above factors serve to keep companies and institutions in line, and act as an effective deterrent to breaches of the environmental trust.

STATUS TODAY: EVALUATION, ADJUSTMENT, MOVING FORWARD

In their Green Plans, the Dutch did not argue against economic growth. Rather they concentrated on managing the negative impacts on nature and health with the principle that a rise in one need not automatically result in a rise in the other. They call that "decoupling."[8] So while economic growth should continue to rise, emission would have to go down in absolute terms. This decoupling has been achieved for all emissions except for carbon dioxide. In many cases the pace of the trends going down is even sufficient for reaching the targets. It is clear now that some of the goals have not been met, some things haven't been achieved, and parts of the goal have had to be adjusted and given a more realistic time frame. It is a matter of adjustment within the overall context of the goal, toward which the country is steadily moving.

The assessment in their Fourth National Policy Plan was that by keeping up the momentum many problems would be solved within the established timeframes. The RIVM data supported that assessment, especially for those problems for which

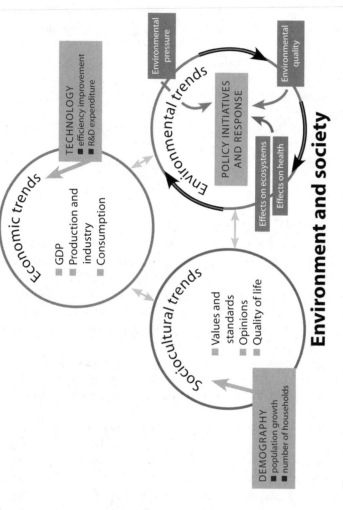

Fig. 4. Environment and society: schematic presentation of the interactions between societal trends and the environmental chain (*Environmental Balance 2004*, The Netherlands: National Institute for Public Health and the Environment, 2004, 4)

there are easy and not too costly alternatives, or technology issues that are about to be solved.[9] Still, some sticky, persistent problems remain; many of these problems are closely related to our addiction to energy, unlimited mobility, and the way in which we feed and nourish ourselves. Issues like sustainable energy, health, sustainable agriculture, and improved transportation practices are complex and interrelated and take much more time to accomplish compared to easier matters like solid waste, which have been solved. This is not surprising, nor discouraging. With all the other pressures both within and without the country, can you really solve carbon emissions in twenty-five years? Can you totally recover fisheries in twenty-five years? In these, and in several other sectors, the Dutch have realized that some issues are going to have to slide over the deadline. Maybe it will take forty to fifty years for problems such as those that involve investment with a long lifespan, like energy and transportation systems.

Postponing does not mean they are capitulating or giving up on, say, fisheries. The point is that they continue to look at the overall condition, within which fisheries make up one part; and that part may improve more slowly than another part, such as water quality. By sustaining the long view, and being alert to but not blinded by specific criticisms, the Dutch keep making progress. Successful in some areas and not so successful in others, they're achieving the central idea with which they started; progress can be seen and measured. To an observer looking back over eighteen years, I marvel at the fact that the NEPP is still functioning and has achieved much of what it set out to do, which seemed an imposing goal at the time.

BRIEF SUMMARY OF PROGRESS TO DATE

As the RIVM report shows, progress has been made in many areas. While the Dutch economy continues to grow steadily, emissions are going down, even in absolute terms. The decoupling of economic growth and emissions is actually taking place. At the same time, it is clear that continuous efforts are needed to reach their goals. The RIVM report clearly illustrates which problems are safely solved and which ones are remain problematical.

Markers of progress can be shown in many ways for very different problems. For example, eighteen years ago, the Rhine was one of Europe's most polluted rivers. Today, thanks to concerted efforts by the countries through which it flows, the levels of toxins have dropped by more than half. Some toxins, including dioxins and DDT, have been completely eliminated. Others have been considerably reduced. Salmon have returned to the Rhine and habitat is improving. In the delta area of the Netherlands, contamination levels from industrial dumping is being cleaned up, but agricultural runoff, as well as pharmaceutical residues, continues to accumulate, posing a complicated problem.[10]

The goal set for noise reduction has nearly been achieved, and plans continue to improve it. In 2003, the Ministry of Public Works and Water Management began an innovative campaign for noise reduction from traffic, including a combination of "smart applications" such as "quieter asphalt," "quieter tires," noise-blocking road embankments, and "whispering trains." Because of budget restraints, the goal for completion of these measures has been extended.[11]

Although air quality has improved, it remains a problem throughout Europe. The three ingredients most difficult to remove stem from auto exhaust; they include particulate matter, ground-level ozone, and nitrogen dioxide. These pollutants are all known to be detrimental to health; however, specific science is lacking as to what levels and what combinations are clearly harmful and in what ways they affect people and the ecosystem. Lacking clarification of the exact toxic effects has made it extremely difficult to impose the costly restrictions that would bring these pollutant levels closer to the goal.

Still the Dutch have recently entered into an experiment to control air pollution by reducing speed on the motorways.

They've set an eighty-kilometers-per-hour (forty-five miles per hour) limit on several of their busier major motorways after having found that cars traveling at high speeds burn fuel less efficiently and therefore spew more emissions into the air.[12] The result in the affected areas is that pollution is down by 10 percent and noise has been reduced by nearly half. There is renewed debate in the Netherlands on environment and health because the Council of State has been turning down construction plans since the Dutch have been having difficulty meeting the European standards for air quality. Additional measures are called for and the Dutch Cabinet has adopted reduced speed limits and new fiscal incentives to promote cleaner diesel use. Without a national automobile industry the Netherlands is one of the strongest advocates in the EU of more stringent standards for automobile engines.

In a small country subject to intense population and industrial pressures landscape will always be threatened. You can go into the great art museums in the Netherlands and see all the Dutch masterpieces with bountiful landscapes, hunting parties going out, and tables full of game. None of that is in existence anymore. Why? This outcome is the result of population pressures as well as a whole range of other issues affecting quality of life and the way people think and act.

In recent history, the Dutch landscape has given way to modernized agriculture and industry, and now it has to compete with the ever-present encroachment of housing and other urban development. Need for development and desire for conservation and the accompanying quality of life coexist and sometimes coincide in this small nation.

At the same time, movement toward the goal, slow in parts, faster in others, continues moving forward. Streams and rivers are improving and forest areas are expanding, but eutrophication (the gradual enrichment of a body of water with dissolved nutrients, which in term stimulates the growth of aquatic plant life, leading to oxygen depletion) continues to be a problem.

Health of species varies. For example, meadow birds as well as two-thirds of the country's butterfly species are suffering, but bats are doing well.[13]

The government's National Spatial Strategy and Agenda for a Living Countryside Policy is working to identify and preserve certain national landscapes possessing "core qualities" such as openness, landforms, field patterns, parcelization, and water courses. The National Ecological Network (NEN) was established in 1990 to create a network of interconnected nature reserves and conservation areas by 2018. The NEN continues, but on a limited budget and with less governmental support. According to the Natura 2000 (a European network of protected sites) and NEN April 2004 reports, nearly 10 percent of Dutch land area has been designated as conservation areas. Developing new green recreational areas has slacked off in recent years although it has long been a goal. There are many groups involved in the effort to preserve landscape and create green areas; however, a major problem, as reported by the RIVM, is the rezoning of areas for development with the attendant rise in property values.

In order to save money, the central government transfers authority to the provinces to oversee the preservation effort. One of the strengths of the Dutch management approach is allowing the provinces to carry out the government's objective as they see fit. The provinces must report on their progress each year; therefore, the annual reports are very important. The demand for land and the desire for natural landscape are both real so provinces have to develop plans that balance the two. How well they balance will be seen over time.

THE POLITICAL BASIS OF THE NEPP

One of the strongest proponents for comprehensive environmental reform has been Queen Beatrix. In her 1988 Christmas address to the nation, she warned that, "The earth is slowly dying, and the inconceivable—the end of life itself—is actually becoming conceivable." It was a shocking and heartfelt speech, concluding that "the future of creation itself is at stake," and calling for no less than a revolution in which the environmental condition would be reviewed and "our way of life adjusted accordingly."[14]

The message carried special impact since earlier that year, in her annual address on the state of the nation, the queen had said that the Netherlands' environment was actually improving. That speech had been written, as usual, by the staff of the prime minister, Christian Democrat Rudd Lubbers. The claim was clearly not consistent with observable reality, and raised many eyebrows. When Lubbers was asked for data to back up his claim, not surprisingly, he and his staff were unable to provide it.

Every citizen could see the magnitude of the environmental problem. They saw that the few fish left in the Rhine were inedible, the fees they paid for drinking water and waste collection were constantly going up, and that traffic jams had become, and still are, a way of life as the number of cars continues to increase. The Netherlands government had been working on a system of environmental controls in a piecemeal way since the early eighties, but with little effect. Momentum was hampered by conflict and resistance to change. Solving one problem sometimes gave rise to other problems. Further, the effort lacked a system of checks to measure progress against the lofty goal.

The RIVM had been working for three years on an intensive review of the environmental issue and in 1989 published its findings in a report entitled *Concern for Tomorrow*. This report, like the queen's speech, formed another milestone on the road to social awakening. After an exhaustive study of the sources, projected increases, and tolerable levels of pollution, the RIVM concluded that the measures in place since the early eighties were insufficient and unless the government adapted their recommendations the environment was facing irreversible damage. The report became a major media event and, like the queen's speech, underlined the need for urgent action. In response, the National Environmental Policy Plan (NEPP) was launched.

Concern for Tomorrow looked at three scenarios for the future: one that would simply be a continuation of current policy, one that would involve only moderately stronger measures, and one that would solve the problems as we know them today. It concluded that, from the scientific point of view, the country should attempt the third scenario. In assessing the changes needed, the RIVM did not only look at the environmental part of the equation. The costs for society as a whole were also assessed. The costs needed were remarkably bearable and clearly helped to shape public support.

The Dutch realized that from an environmental perspective the third scenario was most favorable, as it solved the problems structurally. The results in that scenario would not include the risk that growth of income and production would outrun the efficiency gains of technology. However, in economic terms, the third scenario included the uncertainty of the development of energy prices and it was unknown if other countries would formulate policy with a similar ambition. Significantly, they formulated emission reductions of 70-90 percent for nearly all emissions.

SUPPORT FOR THE PLAN

In addition to broad popular support for environmental reform, the principal parties in the Netherlands, from right to left have, since the RIVM report, been in agreement that the country needed a comprehensive plan. Four factors gave the government the political power it needed in order to pass the first NEPP. These factors include a public that was responsive to the issue, a queen who was an inspiring leader and spokesperson, and support from parliament across all party boundaries as well as business.

Without the complete buy-in of many industries, these three would not have been able to hold the plan together and move it forward. The kind of change required had to involve and affect the whole fabric of society. The economic sector, the industrial sector, and the public at large all needed to share the recognition of the problem, to accept the comprehensive plan, and to agree to share benefits and responsibilities over the long term. Public support for the plan itself continues to be very strong. In fact, it is now so deeply rooted in the Dutch political system that it is no longer controversial. This does not mean that the Dutch take public support for granted. Throughout the years they have made continuous efforts to understand the motives of consumers and citizens and fine-tune their message. Clearly they have understood that it is not just a matter of selling policy but also of involving citizens in policy formulation.

With many "close-to-home" problems being solved and the economy going down, the environment is no longer in the top five of most pressing concerns, but it has held a steady place in the top ten. With increasing concerns about the health hazards of fine particulate emissions from automobiles, there is a growing momentum for environmental policy. The Christian democrats have told their politicians recently that environmental protection and sustainable development is number one of the issues that require more attention from their cabinet.

The first test of support of the Dutch Plan came when, as a starting place, parliament selected a proposal to end the subsidies that car commuters then enjoyed. Green Plan advocates argued that if the goal was to get people out of their cars, it was essential to stop subsidizing their driving to work. The proposal was voted down, the government collapsed, the prime minister resigned, and a new government was formed. When the question was put to the people, they voted overwhelmingly to pursue the NEPP on the scale it was intended.

CONSENSUS IS KEY

Since that time, the country has reached a high level of consensus about what should happen, such as how much money is spent and how goals are to be achieved. It is not likely to matter now if a different leader or party takes over the government. The new conservative cabinet, despite the difficult economic situation, did not question the overall ambitions of their NEPP4. They announced that these ambitions would be maintained yet they set more clear priorities and placed more emphasis on market-based instruments. Understandably, the cabinet placed an even stronger emphasis on European policy to ensure a level playing field for Dutch enterprises. For a limited number of problems, they changed the time frame in which they should be resolved; however the overall ambition and approach remained firm. In fact, the policy document itself was called "Permanent Values, New Forms," which reflects continuity and flexibility. This continuity and flexibility is part of the reason why the Dutch Plans work. Everyone profits from understanding that there are long-term ambitions remaining stable year after year, and implementation strategies that can be adjusted as they move along. Their goals are firm but their plans are not cast in stone.

One thing I have seen in my years of observing and participating in government policymaking is that for something to be accomplished there has to be a buy-in on the part of government employees. You may think you're making headway, but if there is a lot of opposition, it will only last until you are replaced, whereby it disappears. On the other hand, if your plan has a great deal of appeal, such as the Green Plans have in the Netherlands, the public employees "lay it on a track" once they get it, and they are going to be there a lot longer than you. Frustrated managers, who can't get anything to change, call it a "track in stone." You can't just rub it out. If something is in stone, and things are flowing through it, it's there. It has become part of behavior and is accepted, and it will be defended. That's how I see the Green Plans in the Netherlands.

For example, in Amsterdam, soon after the first NEPP, a colleague of mine asked a cab driver what he thought of his country's national environmental plan. "Just another way for the government to increase the taxes on the poor working man," came the grumbling reply. Asked if it had no benefit for him, he answered, "Well, not so much, but it will my children, and that is what is important."

Now, after eighteen years, a visiting Dutch official told me that Green Plans are so deeply rooted in Dutch political consciousness that, if anything, it may be in danger of being taken for granted. Their NEPP4 observes that with the "managerial" approach to solving environmental issues, the public at large comes to view the changes needed as technical. With a focus on emission reduction targets, for example, appreciation for the real reasons for environmental improvements dwindles. The Dutch NEPP4 clearly (re)states the ambition in general terms: "Environmental policy should contribute toward a safe and healthy life within an attractive living environment and surrounded by dynamic nature areas, without depleting natural resources at present, elsewhere and in the future."[15] In short, environmental protection underpins the quality of life.

TO CHOOSE OR TO LOSE

The Dutch NEPP is titled "To Choose or to Lose" in order to emphasize the fact that we are at the point where our very survival depends on the tough choices we have to make. Policies of waste will not suffice in the long term. Although they may seem to postpone disaster for a few years, the costs of inaction are high, or, more positively, the benefits of action may not be fully understood. "To Choose or to Lose" means that the Dutch understand they must choose a good long-term policy today if they do not want to lose out in the end. The NEPP4's title, "Where There's a Will, There's a World," shows that the determination continues. Despite obstacles, setbacks, and inconsistencies, the challenge, the intention, and the Plan are moving forward.

THE PHILOSOPHICAL BASIS FOR THE NEPP

The Netherlands' comprehensive, integrated approach to environmental planning did not happen overnight. Like most Western countries, the Dutch first began passing environmental legislation in the early 1970s. This first wave of environmental law aimed at single issues such as regulating toxins, cleaning up wastes, and so on. The United States, and most of the world, has continued to use this single-issue approach, but in the 1980s, the Netherlands and a few other nations began to realize that it was not working. The Dutch found that the single-issue approach might generate a very good air-quality policy and still end up with a very bad waste policy, basically just shuffling problems around in the environment, like sweeping trash under the rug. They saw that a better future would lie in crossing the barrier of single-issue approaches to create an integrated approach. This realization is the basis of the success of the Green Plan concept, that the whole package of issues needs to be managed all together. I believe, and the Dutch are proving, that this comprehensive approach is the way to successful natural-resource management for humanity' future.

THE BRUNDTLAND REPORT

The Netherlands' earliest attempts at long-term planning were known as the "Indicative Multi-Year Programs" and were begun in the early 1980s. There were about ten programs altogether, each dealing with different issues, such as noise, soil, air, water, and waste, over a policy lifespan of about five years. These plans together served as an agenda for what ought to happen in the near future to change the quality of life in each particular medium. However, even as the programs were established, the Dutch realized that a more comprehensive, unified approach was required. One important catalyst was the United Nations' World Commission on Environment and Development and its 1987 report *Our Common Future*, better known as the Brundtland Report.[16] This report was an important and clear philosophical statement that has had a major effect on the environmental thinking of most Western nations, and particularly on the Dutch. It was not helpful in a practical way, but rather in forming the idea of sustainability as a concept and goal. That is, development that is sufficient for our needs, but does not harm the environment's carrying capacity or ability to renew itself, thus enabling future generations to enjoy the same prosperity we do.

While the final Dutch NEPP is distinctly its own, part of it was a response to the Brundtland Report. While the Brundtland material did not translate into practical, workable policy, the Dutch found the concept of sustainable development useful as a way of helping them set goals for environmental recovery. They used the Brundtland Commission's concept of solidarity between generations—that is, recognizing each generation's responsibility to manage the environment in a way that sustains it for the next generation. A key theme of the NEPP is that each generation cleans up. This concept of sustainability across generations is at the core of the NEPP, along with two other crucial components. These two components are (a) a comprehensive, cross-boundary approach guided by long-term quantitative targets, as I have described, and (b) the integration of environmental issues into other fields of policymaking.

INTEGRATION OF ENVIRONMENTAL ISSUES INTO POLICYMAKING

One of the tools the Dutch used to develop their integrated approach was a century-old law called the Nuisance Act. This law was originally designed to deal with disturbances, such as noise or odors, which any human activity might create in a community. However, it did not consider such things as noise or odors in terms of the environment.

In the late 1980s, the Dutch began to transform the Nuisance Act into the centerpiece of their integrated approach. Its new form states that a single facility, such as a factory or other business, should be considered in terms of its total impact on the environment. In other words, it requires consideration of a facility's impact in the context of the goals for clean air, clean water, clean soil, and so on, before a permit is drafted for that facility.

INTEGRATION LEADS TO THE NEPP

The eventual outcome of the move toward integration was the National Environmental Policy Plan, which was presented to parliament in its final form by the Lubbers government in 1989. The NEPP contained 223 policy changes aimed at reducing pollution and establishing an economy based on sustainable practices. It was designed as a single, coherent, comprehensive policy that integrates all environmental areas and is based on an ecosystem approach. With the implementation of the NEPP, the Dutch no longer simply react to a single incident, but instead consider what goals their society as a whole are trying to attain.

NEPP policies cut across governmental and social lines and deal with all environment-related policy fields such as economy, energy, agricultural, physical planning, and so on. The NEPP deals with all sectors of society as well, based on the premise that all of society, not just the government, is responsible for cleaning up the environment and preventing pollution. Every single actor contributes to the problem, and therefore each is a stakeholder in the recovery process and is responsible for the solutions in proportion to its share of responsibility. This approach is fairly new to the field of environmental policymaking and encourages more complex and sophisticated solutions to environmental problems. That the NEPP continues to work over time is evidenced in the RIVM summary of 2004, which notes that many groups are now getting involved in conserving nature, including some which before would have seemed to be adversaries. As the Green Plan has become a national behavior habit, even developers and farmers are participating in the government's environmental effort.

KEEPING UP-TO-DATE

Comprehensive environmental planning is a process, not a one-time effort, and for that reason the NEPP is updated every four years. The first update was the National Environmental Policy Plan Plus (+), covering the years 1990 to 1994. Early in 1994, the second version of the NEPP was published. While the first NEPP set out the main objectives of Dutch environmental policy, the second NEPP focused on carrying out the first Plan's initiatives and ensuring that its goals were met. Core elements of NEPP+ included strengthening the implementation framework, introducing follow-up measures where targets are not being met, and working toward sustainable patterns of production and consumption. International diplomacy and issues of economic development played a larger role in the NEPP+. In March of 1995, parliament reviewed the NEPP+ and ratified it with overwhelming support from both parties and from all sectors of the public. This ongoing confirmation by parliament is a very important step in securing the future of the NEPP in Dutch society.

The NEPP+ was partly criticized because it did not address the perceived necessary changes within the economic system. Opposition in parliament argued that lack of progress in meeting the targets was due to economic growth in many of the intense industry sectors of the Netherlands. Left-wing opposition argued that the growth of the steel, chemistry, glasshouse agriculture, intensive cattle breeding, and (freight) transport businesses had to be slowed down. The Dutch Cabinet did not adhere to that view, but promised a Policy Document on Environment and Economy. This document was published in 1997. The basis for it was a strong statement in the new cabinet's strategic Government Policy Agreement. It states: "[T]he future of our economy is more than a matter of costs. The requirement for sustainability changes the concept of economic growth. Depleting our physical environment must make way for drawing on our reserves of inventiveness and creativity. Economy and ecology must co-exist."[17] The Dutch Plan describes many imaginative projects for achieving more efficient environmental production in different sectors of the economy. More importantly it establishes a framework for promoting these positive examples. Fiscal incentives, greening the tax system, shifting taxes away from direct labor taxes to environmental taxation, and greening public procurement and investment policy were seen as the key instruments. They were seen as key instruments not as driven from a "blueprint" of the economy but to gear market dynamism to eco-efficiency and gains for both the economy and the environment.

The NEPP3 mainly consolidated widespread and ongoing environmental efforts. Working parallel to the Policy Document on Environment and Economy, it stressed the importance of using market dynamism to solve environmental problems. Getting prices right and greening the taxation system were key points in the NEPP3. The Dutch have a remarkable track record on greening the taxation system. A large part of their tax income, almost fourteen billion euros, comes from "green taxes."[18] Among their green taxes is a carbon dioxide tax for households and small energy users, and taxes on water supply, waste, and uranium. Their Central Economic Planning Agency recommends making even more use, at the appropriate level, of instruments in line with market conditions, like emissions trading and levies.

The NEPP3 analyzed the reasons for success in curbing emission trends. They found that broad public support and cooperation with target groups was crucial. They learned that the problems most successfully tackled were relatively unequivocal and related to a limited number of large emission sources. For dispersed problems from many different sources, like pesticide use, success was more difficult to grasp. Other problems, such as increasing number of automobiles, were caused by the volume of economic growth. Their assessment was that bigger leaps in technological progress are needed to solve these problems. The NEPP4 was their response to that assessment.

The NEPP4 clearly marked the success of previous NEPP efforts and formulated a new way of dealing with the "persistent" economic problems that seemed hard to manage. The NEPP4 concluded that many problems were well on the way to being solved and that continuation of the efforts guided by the NEPP3 would enable meeting the 2010 targets. At the same time, it concluded that some "old" problems remained hard to tackle and new problems kept arising. Learning from almost twelve years of experience of policy implementation, it was clear that the reasons environmental policy is necessary should be communicated with wider appeal. Whereas long-term targets are a crucial element of the Dutch management approach, they cloud the real reasons for effective environmental policy as a contribution to the quality of life and an "insurance policy" for a safe future.

The NEPP4 addressed these persistent problems from a comprehensive view called "transition," an approach designed to answer the question of how to foster the fundamental changes needed to ensure desired long-term environmental quality. Their idea of transition comes from the observation that more fundamental changes are needed in the way people's needs are met. Small efficiency gains are outrun by growth of volume, so the Dutch decided that managing whole systems, such as transport and energy systems, is needed.

Transition management requires that the government learn to deal with uncertainty, partly by using scenarios, partly by paying attention to the international dimension of certain processes, and also by keeping options open as long as possible. The notion of keeping options open does not refer to doing nothing and waiting for a magic moment in which problems are solved. It refers to the fact that many different technological options may contribute to solving the problem and that choosing one option might hinder the full development of other promising options. As government clearly is not good at picking winners, they had better set market conditions and establish dialogue with stakeholders to foster the changes needed.

Abstract as this notion of transition may seem, in practice the Dutch try to figure out how the different parts of the puzzle of economic, technological, sociocultural, and institutional changes fit together and promote the changes needed. They promote changes not as abstract ambition but as a path to realizing a low-carbon energy supply, sustainable agriculture, and a life without health risks from chemical substances in the Netherlands. They also do not turn a blind eye to the rest of the world. They clearly define their share in solving the problems that occur elsewhere and later.

The NEPP4 thus continues to take a long-view approach by planning up to 2030, while addressing the more immediate issues as well in setting quantitative and qualitative objectives or target groups. Even more strongly than before, the NEPP4 guides these changes not only from a technical-physical perspective but from a comprehensive view encompassing all the pieces of the puzzle of societal change. I will look with interest to the results over the coming years.

In addition to the national Green Plan, the government has required each of the twelve provinces to write a plan for its jurisdiction, with an update every four years. Provinces in the Netherlands are not sovereign, as are Canada's, but they do have regional jurisdiction. The provinces are, for the most part, responsible for the implementation and enforcement of local and regional environmental policies, and for keeping the government informed annually of the conditions they are responsible for maintaining.

Over the years, the Dutch have had to adjust to changes and to unexpected advances and obstacles they hadn't considered. They're dealing with a comprehensive package of all the factors involved in the environment, and in the economy for that matter. So it's important to keep the overall vision in sight, because then you can adjust en route. Their Green Plan is stable in its long-term ambitions and flexible in its implementation, with the demands on industry remaining consistent and transparent throughout the years.

Think of it this way. An inventor designs a new technology intending that it will work, and work well. The Dutch have designed their environmental Plan with the same intent. The planning process in many of the developed nations has become an excuse for not making a political decision, or for putting off tough decisions. However, when a government makes 223 genuine policy changes, as the Dutch have done, and the voters back it up, and continue to back it up, as Dutch voters have done, the nation has made a serious commitment to change. The Plan moves forward, and its design gets adjusted throughout the years so that political, societal, and economic changes can be accommodated without losing sight of the final ambition. Such a program provides an excellent model of a progressive nation implementing a well-functioning, working environmental plan leading to a sustainable society.

CAVEAT

As a cautionary note, I think it's important to observe that as a policymaker, one has to keep one's eye on the broad view. The job of academics and scientists is to drill down into detail, to examine at the level of the "nano bit," but in so doing they risk losing the whole picture. When you look in a comprehensive way at the total environment and take a snapshot of how it looks at this one given moment, because of the very wide breadth of it, we have to remember that there are constant changes going on; even as you read this, sometimes unpredictable, sometimes negative, and sometimes very positive changes are happening. A case in point is the total shifting of gears in the practice of destroying solid waste. The Dutch had been forbidden to burn it, since the resulting smoke was so toxic, and had become expert at recycling. Suddenly, new technology was developed and they realized they could actually filter the smoke from the burning. Now they recycle critical parts of the waste, newspapers and so on, and then burn the rest safely, by filtering the smoke and converting that energy to fuel. Not long after solving their solid-waste issues, the Dutch realized that their real waste problem was how to deal with greenhouse gas emissions. An example of an obstacle to solving this problem is that the Dutch rather naively thought their carbon dioxide goals could be easily accomplished. But they haven't been, and it remains a problem, but it is problematic for everyone else too.

Cleaning up farm soils has turned out to be a lot more expensive than expected and hard to do because the Dutch had to develop the technology to do it. This is a great example of how they have learned in practice that it would have been up to ten times cheaper to prevent the problem in the first place than to clean it up later.

Certain deadlines have had to be extended, but to the Dutch this is just part of planning. It's not a scientific or technical concept you're looking at, it's a philosophical goal down the road. They have twenty-five years to totally recover environmental quality at every level. This goal makes politicians accountable, as success and failure is clear to everyone. The on-going debate about the progress and practicalities informs the course for the future. All the while, it is the overall plan, leading to the long-term goal, which is important.

When dealing with a long-term goal of this magnitude, keeping track along the way is crucial. Every four years they look ahead as part of the preparations for a new National Environmental Policy Plan. Visualizing scenarios makes them aware of possible obstacles and gives clear insight as to costs and benefits. Monitoring is always done with an eye on the overall objectives, and as I've described, the stability and flexibility of that long-term framework gives them room to maneuver. While policy goals may not necessarily need to be changed year to year, needed changes are seriously considered. If you keep your eye on the vision, the ultimate goal, then on the one hand you don't give up, and on the other hand you don't get overly enthusiastic; you're just being realistic.

It takes political courage to be willing to be held so accountable. I have never seen a government stand up and say so clearly, when it is the case, "We failed at this." They are brave enough to reveal what they are doing, in a way that every citizen can easily understand, to show a line on a graph that should go down and does not, or is not going down as fast as you would like it to go down. They are very open and honest, and that takes a great deal of political courage.

THE STRUCTURE OF THE NEPP PROCESS

The first Dutch National Environmental Policy Plan analyses the root causes of environmental degradation in physical terms and outlines three particularly important mechanisms for making sustainability achievable: (a) integrated lifecycle management, (b) energy conservation, and (c) improved product quality. General goals in regard to these, such as doubling the lifespan of products and stabilizing the use of energy by the year 2000, are stated in the Plan.

Integrated lifecycle management goes beyond simple recycling or reuse programs; it is really about closing economic cycles and resource-use cycles in a way that makes them sustainable. There are many graphs, flow charts, and illustrations in the Plan about cycles and leaks and contributions, but what it all boils down to is reducing the quantity of materials used by industry across the board.

Energy conservation is also essential to sustainability, since developed nations are now using energy at a rate that will use up current supplies within a few generations. The Dutch initially set aside about $385 million per year for energy conservation for the first four years.[19] Ideas like cogeneration, using the energy from production for heating purposes, are popular in the Netherlands.

The third mechanism is improving product quality, so that products themselves have a longer lifetime and are easier to recycle or dispose of when they are no longer usable. For example, the Dutch government now requires the auto industry to take responsibility for what happens to their cars when their useful lives are over. Among other things, this has forced the manufacturers to figure out what can be done at the drawing-board stage to ensure that it is easier to dispose of an old car.

It is challenges like these that bring out innovative thinking. For instance, Volkswagen made one small change that has helped a great deal. It marks all the different types of plastics it uses in the car, so that when it is demolished it is easy to tell what type of plastic the bumper is, for example, and sort it appropriately. This means that much more of the plastic in old Volkswagens can now be reused. Before, when the plastics were mixed, it was difficult and costly to reprocess them or they could only be used in low-quality products.

These challenges have also led to the development of innovative planning tools. For instance, the Dutch government has established a fifty-year program for developing sustainable technology that does something called "backcasting." Backcasting, a longstanding practice in management planning, looks ahead to a goal, to be finalized, say, in the year 2040, and considers what needs to be done to get there, how long the various steps will take, and then works backward to where you are, so that you are laying out a general path to be followed.

The approach the Dutch have taken to tackle the remaining "persistent" environmental problems as laid out in their NEPP4 is similar. The underlying idea is that the remaining problems are closely related to production and consumption processes for which there is no easy substitute. For these problems a long-term goal sets the direction, and the practical steps will follow.

IMPORTANT PRINCIPLES OF THE FIRST NATIONAL ENVIRONMENTAL POLICY PLAN

There are a number of fundamental principles the Dutch have adopted in order to achieve sustainability, and which are incorporated into the first NEPP. These are:

- The stand-still principle (environmental quality may not deteriorate)
- Abatement at the source (remove causes rather than ameliorate effects)
- The polluter pays principle (the user of a resource pays for the negative effects of that use)
- Prevention of unnecessary pollution
- Application of the best practicable means (following the development of abatement technology)
- Carefully controlled waste disposal
- Application of a two-track policy of more stringent source-oriented measures on effect-oriented quality standards
- Internalization of environmental concerns (motivating people to responsible behavior)[20]

Some of these principles are well known and widely accepted. Planners in our own country and in other developed nations agree that they are important principles, but they rarely, if ever, apply them. Certainly their efforts are not comparable to what the Dutch have done in integrating all eight principles into one plan. Every instrument of the Dutch Plan is required to take each of these principles into consideration, which is quite tough to carry out politically and is the reason it has not been done before. The Netherlands' willingness to face such difficult political decisions shows that it and other Green Plan nations are for the first time becoming as serious about sustainability and survival as the superpowers have been about economic and technological power.

Although the principles listed above may seem simple in theory, their application is extremely complex and requires a diverse array of approaches to address each pollution source in the country. For example, everyone would probably agree that unnecessary pollution should be prevented, but what are the "best practical means" for achieving that? In addition, the government's definition of unnecessary pollution will almost certainly be different from that of industry, and each side will propose a different way of dealing with it. This debate may prove not to be very constructive as well. If legislation and permits describe the means and the technology to be used, one might indeed get bogged down in lengthy discussion and run the big risk that in the end, yesterday's technology becomes tomorrow's standard. That is why in their licensing the Dutch increasingly prescribe the goals to be achieved. They leave it to the better knowledge and technological insight of industry to find ways to achieve these goals. With fiscal incentives and innovative policy they keep pushing the market not only to develop new technology but to use it on a wide scale.

ACTION CREATES SOCIAL CHANGE

The NEPP4 analyzed the causes of environmental problems from a perspective of societal change. It identified seven reasons why persistent problems remain unsolved. The planners concluded that problems can be solved, but that it doesn't pay to solve them. Parties involved in an environmental issue often have insufficient interest in solving it. This happens first because short-term thinking prevails and is not sufficiently counterbalanced by incentives aimed at long-term solutions. Policy responses are fragmented and markets send the wrong signals. This is even more cumbersome as the long-term investments needed are often risky investments, given the uncertainty of future developments. This may lead to a wait-and-see attitude, sluggishness, and delaying tactics. As long-term costs and benefits are taken into account, all such obstacles will lead to lack of precaution.

The NEPP4 attempts to tackle these problems. For example, principle 6 addressed the problem of "carefully controlled waste disposal" by creating a policy that no waste shall be exported; whatever is produced in the Netherlands must be taken care of there. This is a renunciation of the practice of some countries of shipping their trash to poor nations and dumping it for a fee.

Principle 7, the "two-track approach," using both effect-oriented and source-oriented techniques, is primarily about flexibility. According to this principle, some problems are better handled from an effect-oriented perspective, which means applying clean-up technology, and some are better handled by source-oriented means, which focus on pollution prevention.

The Dutch have largely focused their efforts on source orientation, which is much more efficient in the long run, but they still use many effect-oriented measures, especially in terms of safeguarding environmental quality standards in a specific area. Any plan or policy must comply with the water-quality standards of the water board, or with the air-quality standards, which are national, or with the soil protection criteria.

Another key principle is that of "internalization," which means that people must consider beforehand whether or not any decision they make or action they take will be consistent with environmental policy. It is probably the hardest principle to apply, asking CEO's or plant managers to take into consideration all of the principles listed above in the way they deal with all the environmental problems on their plates. The Dutch not only demand this of business, the same is required of government officials and their departments.

The principles of the first National Environmental Policy Plan underpinned many of the actions defined in that plan and continue to guide policy. Further plans laid out general principles in relation to the focus of that specific plan. The NEPP+ very much focused on the implementation of the actions of the first NEPP. Successful implementation called for three basic conditions. First, identification of a clear and complete set of targets so that every sector has a consistent set of demands over time. The NEPP+ thus expanded the target-group approach to other sectors, and completed the set of targets and tasks for each sector where they had not yet been set. The second condition was to strengthen the development and application of technology and cleaner products as crucial conditions for changes needed. Last, it called for a common understanding of priorities for the years to come. Taking the differences of sectors into account, they called it "customized implementation."

PLANNING BY SCALE AND THEME:
MANAGEMENT INNOVATION

The Dutch use a five-level model of geographic scale to provide a framework for managing environmental problems. This model reflects the fact that every environmental problem originates on a particular geographic scale, and each solution is also located on a specific geographic level, although they are not always the same. The five scales they have defined, which come from the scientific report *Concern for Tomorrow*, are: local, regional, fluvial (watershed), continental, and global.

The National Environmental Policy Plan also sets targets and goals for specific policy issues, or "themes," that are to be addressed at each geographic level. These themes also come from *Concern for Tomorrow*, which asserted that they were the crucial issues for the future. They include:

- Climate change (the greenhouse effect, damage to the ozone layer)
- Acidification
- Eutrophication
- Toxic and hazardous substance pollution
- Waste disposal (solid waste, radioactive waste, sewerage, soil clean-up)
- Nuisance (noise, odor, safety)
- Dehydration (water depletion and the draining of wetlands)
- Squandering (depletion of soil and other natural resources)

An example of a problem on the global level is the issue of climate change. Although the Netherlands would be greatly affected by global warming, with 27 percent of its countryside below sea level and almost 50 percent of its land less than one meter above sea level, it cannot solve the problem of climate change by itself.[21] If other nations do not follow its example, the Netherlands is doomed. That is why it is so heavily involved in environmental education and negotiation at the diplomatic level.

Such problems as transboundary pollution from air toxins are continental in scale; acidification is one example. The NEPP's strategies to combat acidification focus on enforcing stringent emission standards for all the sources that contribute to acid rain, such as auto exhaust, coal-burning plants, and so on. Other strategies promote reductions in neighboring countries, because most of the airborne toxins in the Netherlands come from somewhere else, just as many of its emissions end up somewhere else. If the Netherlands reduces its emissions, it does not help its own clean-up that much, although it does help Norway's air quality.

Almost every country has problems with airborne toxins that drift in from other places, so international cooperation on this and other environmental issues is crucial. That is why there are treaties like that of the UN Economic Commission for Europe on transboundary pollution and acidifying compounds. This treaty covers all of Europe, dealing with these issues and seeing that each country does its share, and in the end everyone contributes and everyone benefits.

The Netherlands does not really have fluvial problems apart from the Rhine River basin, but that is probably one of the biggest issues it faces. Since 1998, as part of a united effort of European countries to restore the Rhine as a whole ecosystem, the river has been returning to health. Fish have returned. Natural habitats have improved in the delta where toxins have been dumped for centuries, contamination levels are falling, but the task is difficult and progress is slow.

The problem of eutrophication operates on both the fluvial and regional levels. Eutrophication, which is the depletion of oxygen in water sources due to the accumulation of large amounts of nutrients, is usually caused by agricultural runoff and is a big problem in the intensively farmed Netherlands. Most Dutch farmers do not have enough land to dispose of all the manure produced by their animals; it must be treated or processed into products. Part of the NEPP strategy for this theme is to get farmers to cut back on the amount of fertilizer they use, but in the end, they may have to scale back on their numbers of livestock. This, in fact, is happening; the numbers of livestock have fallen steadily since 1980. The number of small farms has fallen off, and the number of large, intensive farms has increased. Nitrogen and phosphate deposits from agriculture have been reduced, but are still too high to meet European standards.

The diffusion of toxic substances in water and soil, another problem that operates on both the fluvial and regional level, is one area in which the Dutch have not yet made a great deal of progress. Pesticides in groundwater and surface water have gone down considerably, but there has been but a slight reduction in pesticides in soil.[22] Farming in the Netherlands is so intensive that there has not been much support for switching to organic farming methods. The government is concentrating now on switching farmers over to less hazardous alternatives and convincing them to use smaller quantities of pesticides.

Much of the country's soil is a type of clay that is quite productive. Unfortunately, clay also holds toxic compounds longer than do sandy soils, and that creates another set of problems. It means that the active compounds in pesticides will trickle down to the groundwater level, and eventually to the drinking water—and some compounds have a lifetime of twenty to thirty years. The Netherlands is encountering drinking-water problems now from substances used decades ago. These are difficult to clean up, and while progress is being made, the target dates have had to be extended.

There are also local problems, like odor and noise, which are important issues in the Netherlands because its population is so dense. However, from 1995 to 2004, noise reduction has improved by just one point, reducing from 44 percent to 43 percent of people aged eighteen or older bothered by the noise.[23] "Stench pollution" however has gone down four points in that time, from 18 percent to 14 percent.[24] Other local problems include indoor environmental pollutants such as asbestos, formaldehyde, and secondhand smoke.

The NEPP sets specific targets for pollution reductions for each theme and at each geographic level. On the fluvial level it aims for 70 to 90 percent reduction in emissions of eutrophic or poorly degradable substances by 2010, while on the regional level it calls for a 70 to 90 percent reduction of eutrophic, acidifying, and nondegradable substances. The size of the waste stream is also to be reduced.

By 2012, only two billion kilos of waste that cannot be burned may be dumped in a landfill. Dumped waste has gone down from fourteen billion kilos in 1990 to three billion kilos in 2003. Recycling has gone up from 55 percent to 80 percent in the same period.[25]

According to the RIVM's *Environmental Balance 2004*, emissions of most pollutants have fallen in recent decades, and air and water quality has improved considerably. Yet, in most cases, improvement will not be enough to meet the European targets for 2010. However, efforts toward climate renewable energy and emissions of ammonia and waste management are currently on target.

If each theme, or problem area, has an appropriate level of scale, so do each of the actions to be taken in response. For example, a problem could have global effects, but if there is only one source, like an accident at a nuclear reactor, then action should be taken at the local level. Rather than treating people for radioactive fallout, it would make far more sense to go to the source of the problem and stop the emissions from the reactor.

The instruments chosen should also be more or less determined by the scale of the problem as well as the nature of the solution. For example, there is no point in putting money into demonstration projects on climate change; it makes more sense to come up with treaties that require every country to cut its emissions a certain amount by such and such a time.

THE TARGET GROUPS

In creating the NEPP, the government wanted to tailor its policies to those social sectors that contributed the most to the problems listed above. Therefore, it selected a set of target groups, most of which are composed of industries in various sectors, that were carefully chosen on the basis of the contributions they make to one or more of the themes.

The key target groups are: agriculture, traffic and transport, industry, the energy sector, building trade, consumers and the retail trade, the environmental trade (water suppliers, the waste sector), research and education, and public organizations. Some of the business-related target groups have been broken down even further into specific business categories, such as the basic metals industry, the packaging industry, and the printing industry. The government has set both general and specific goals for these groups.

Much of the Netherlands' environmental policy is set by means of signed agreements reached between the government and representatives of the various target groups. Often industry representatives are allowed to determine the most efficient way to reach the goals set by the scientists, rather than the government imposing rules that might or might not work.

Long-term goals for each target group are not negotiable, but the methods for getting there are negotiable. The long-term perspective is a very important element of the NEPP approach, and it has been so successful that just about every goal in "To Choose or to Lose" has the blessing of the industries concerned, although there is plenty of fighting over the short-term methods.

The government has encouraged companies within each group to organize their efforts in a trade association to make negotiating and policymaking easier and more efficient. The government realized that if it wanted industry's active cooperation toward environmental goals it would have to make it easier for businesses to work with government. To accomplish this, it appointed a "target-group manager" for each target group as an official in the Ministry of the Environment to whom businesses can bring all their questions and problems regarding environmental issues. The efficiency of this "one mailbox" approach is common to the Green Plan nations. It secures businesses' initial cooperation and convinces them to compromise on a wider range of issues.

There's a saying that there are many parents for any success. In this case there are many "parents" who deserve to be commended, including the government, business, and the nongovernmental organizations (NGOs). The business leadership, for example, believe that they were the essential element that has led to the definition and emergence of the success of the NEPP, and to a great degree that seems to be true. Business provided the initial leadership in many phases. The decision was a break from the narrow practice of close cooperation with certain economic entities, which prefer to ignore environmental problems. Here in the United States, business remains in the grip of such entities, in particular the Chamber of Commerce, with the support of the fossil fuel interests. In the Dutch success, however, instead of holding back environmental progress, business provided a remarkable example of leadership. They had the experience as managers, and they could put the structure together in a workable form, which is why the NEPP idea is so effective. It is a management concept that really works.

I believe such plans will work in the United States and other developed nations because the management concept works and is proving itself successful, as well as leading toward sustainability. However, currently, U.S. business is frustrated by old-style environmental regulations and laws. There is no lack of distrust between industry and government, and between industry and environmental groups. In fact, this distrust is professionally fanned by economic interest groups who want to make sure industry doesn't step back and reveal that a program like the one in Holland would be to their advantage here. While visiting a U.S. state capital, one of my Dutch guests once observed that the Environmental Protection Agency and Chamber of Commerce buildings were literally on opposite sides of the street. It struck him as a very visual symbol of money and ingenuity being spent on litigation and delaying tactics rather than solving problems jointly, in a timely and cost-effective manner, with mutual recognition of different interests.

This same visitor noted that sometimes, while he sees promising signs in the United States, more often he is discouraged to see that when proactive industries step forward, they are blocked by the federal government. The proactive industries recognize that pursuing an environmental agenda is in their interest and that creativity and ingenuity can be applied to problems like climate change, but the current administration's directives hinder cooperation to this end. Rather than designing well-balanced policies that offer environmental improvement without undermining the interests of business, it seems that policy in the United States is designed to support the interests of those friendly to the government and detrimental to the environment. He asked me what could be done to get business out of the defensive litigating mode and into a constructive proactive mode that is rewarded by policy. I referred him back to the example of the Dutch, and I suggested that time and new elections will bring positive changes too.

GREEN PLANS BRING SEEMINGLY OPPOSING INTERESTS TOGETHER

Green Plans offer a workable alternative to the old command-and-control method of establishing and enforcing rules. While approach was useful in developing our nations, as sometimes happens, better discoveries and improved methods, such as the Dutch Green Plans, have recently evolved. With the present complexity of our economy and industries and the interconnected nature of it all, a new, comprehensive model is an improvement. Now, while rules are still in place, greater flexibility has advantages as shown by the Green Plan–nation models. Arguably the biggest factor behind the success of the existing Green Plans has been the willingness of businesses to sit down and negotiate environmental quality goals and regulations, and their willingness to cooperate in putting together a comprehensive plan. In return, nations that adopt these comprehensive environmental strategies will need to help their industries make the changes and maintain their competitiveness. The long-term framework allows time for meeting the new demands and standards. Because they operate with such an open exporting economy, the Dutch keep a very close eye on cost-effectiveness and a level playing field for their industries vis-à-vis their competitors.

However, it has not led them to deny problems, delay solutions, or downplay ambitious policy.

On the microeconomic level, the Dutch do expect shifts in some industries and in the beginning expected to allow some companies to go under, simply because their business is so destructive to the environment that the country no longer wants it. Thus far, however, the government knows of no businesses that have moved to another country or gone bankrupt because of environmental policies.

One of the great advantages to this type of planning approach is that it ensures a relatively stable regulatory environment. As I have said, the Netherlands' environmental policy may be demanding, but it does not spring any sudden surprises on business. Another competitive advantage the NEPP approach offers to business is advancement in the field of environmental technology. In many cases, their companies are on the cutting edge of environmentally sound products and practices, because of the NEPP's strict requirements, and the international market for these technologies is rapidly growing.

The target-group approach to business is a major innovation in environmental policy setting, epitomizing the new type of government-business partnerships that Green Plans promise.

NONINDUSTRIAL TARGET GROUPS

Not all of the NEPP target groups are entirely composed of businesses; some include individuals in their roles as consumers, while others include educational and research institutions, or environmental organizations. These nonindustrial target groups pose their own challenges for the government in terms of developing strong, realistic policies.

For instance, trying to reach consumers as a group, in the way they consume products and services that have a specific impact on the environment, is very different from communicating with other target groups. It is not possible to sit down with individual consumers to negotiate a relationship, as can be done with industry, and consumer groups do not represent consumers in the same way a trade association represents its member companies.

One way the Netherlands government has reached out to consumers is through a massive public information campaign. Although the general public has long been aware that the Netherlands has serious environmental problems, they did not know specifically *what* was wrong or the sources of the problems. They certainly did not realize that they, themselves, were contributing to the problem in the way they used energy and water, or did not separate their waste.

To correct this, several years ago the government established a public information program, using magazines, television, radio, billboards, and leaflets in public libraries and post offices. The campaign took place in three parts. The first focused on awakening a general awareness that there was a problem, the second indicated specifically what the problems were, and the third concentrated on the actions each individual could take to correct the problems.

Some remarkable surveys were done and the results indicated that a large percentage of consumers were willing to do things for the environment because government asked it of them. A very large group was convenience oriented, but willing to change if changes were made easy. Only a small percentage was inspired by the intrinsic value of nature itself. There have been recent studies of citizens' priorities showing that environmental continue to rank high. The Netherlands Ministry of Housing, Spatial Planning, and the Environment (VROM) established a policy program to involve citizens more closely in policy formulation.

This last element of the program focuses on changing the day-to-day behavior of the average citizen to a much greater extent than has been attempted before. They are trying to instill a commitment to stewardship and are giving people the information and tools needed to act on that commitment.

To provide more information to the consumer, the government has adopted programs such as eco-labeling for environmentally friendly products and logos that identify how certain products must be disposed of. The Environmental Advertising Code came into force in 1991, forbidding misleading claims about the environmental friendliness of products.

The Dutch have another target group made up of societal groups, primarily environmental nongovernmental organizations. Labor unions and employer associations are also included in these NGOs. In the Netherlands, as well as in a few other European countries and in Canada, some of these organizations are partially funded by the government to perform their roles as advisors and critics. They play their roles as critics quite well, even though they get some government money; and these groups have no problem suing the government when they think it is necessary. Of course, the relationship is not just adversarial; NGOs also provide advice and education. I met some representatives of Netherlands environmental groups at the Rio Earth Summit, and they were very proud of their country's efforts. They were also puzzled at the lack of progress from pressure by the U.S. environmental movement, noting that we seemed to put most of our energy into buying land to preserve it instead.

Research institutions and educational organizations have also been identified as a target group and asked to adopt programs that reflect the intensified need for environmental research and policymaking.

MONITORING AND UPDATING

One of the NEPP's management strengths is its built-in mechanism for careful monitoring of progress and setbacks, and for the frequent updating of goals and strategies based on this information. The basis of the long-term effort is the NEPP plan itself, a four-hundred-page document detailing all the myriad policy changes, and which is updated every four years. These four-year updates are based on forecasting reports by the RIVM, focusing on projections of what will happen down the road using scenarios to explore possible economic and societal developments. The National Institute for Public Health and the Environment's (RIVM) ongoing evaluation of the whole process and program is another huge factor in the Dutch success. The information they release is trusted by the public. The RIVM reports address the question of whether targets will be met given the expected economic development in the different scenarios and given the planned and agreed policy. Equally important, they assess possible additional measures by examining the cost-effectiveness of all possible measures. Furthermore, they ask such questions as: Should new themes be added? Are there new problems emerging that need to be addressed?

In the second year of any four-year period, a report card on the Plan is published. These report cards are more reflective, looking at what is actually happening and what the implications are for future policy. The first report card came out in 1992, and was a remarkable document, 533 pages long. It looked at such questions as how the Plan is being enforced and how the different measures are contributing to the ultimate goal of solving the problem. These reports are the outside control on what the government is doing. Although the government pays for the reports, the research institute that actually does the reporting is independent and highly respected, and is the same one that wrote *Concern for Tomorrow*. Regular outside audits of its programs give a government a strong management advantage, because every time a manager or official signs a document, he or she knows that it is going to be held up to daylight sometime within the next year, when the reviews are done. Results tend to improve when the people in charge know that they will be held accountable for their decisions.

The honesty of the Netherlands' monitoring and reporting continues to be remarkable. The first four-year NEPP update clearly reflects the complexity of the situation and the importance of the Plan's comprehensiveness. The government manages to deal with the entire package, functioning at a level of thinking that we in the United States have not even begun to comprehend. The update exposes the scientific truth of what is really happening under the program, both good and bad, and there have been plenty of examples of both. Honesty and commitment is part of the reason the public is so strongly behind the Netherlands' Plan, why it understands and has confidence in it.

INNOVATIONS SPRING FROM A COMPREHENSIVE APPROACH

The comprehensive approach has allowed the Dutch to create some innovative new programs. One that has caught the world's attention is the flooding of a part of the farmland they drained a century ago.[26] Previously known for building dikes rather than breaching them, the Dutch plan to eventually restore about six hundred thousand acres of wetlands, with the dual goals of halting the fall of their water table and returning the land to the wildlife that once lived there.

They also have an ambitious plan to plant thousands of acres of forest, as part of their objective to eventually be self-sufficient in timber and to make a contribution to the reduction of carbon dioxide in the atmosphere. Wildlife habitat will be expanded too. These kinds of large-scale projects would be next to impossible without a comprehensive and integrated plan, because they involve several ministries.

Cleaning contaminated soil is another fresh approach the Dutch have adopted. There are serious dangers to environmental health from contaminated soil, where the pollutants have exceeded what is safe for growing crops, or where the toxins have leached into the groundwater. One of the first initiatives the government undertook in partnership with business was to list all sites where the soil had been contaminated and to develop plans for cleaning them up. Although it is a costly process, it will have to be handled as part of their overall budget planning. In the past, the government has funded most of the soil treatment, but in the coming years, polluters and users will contribute more to the costs.

It is encouraging to realize that, while it is not possible to create new soil, it may be possible to clean up soil that has been contaminated. We should never forget that a civilization depends on the vitality of its soil. Although it would have been ten times cheaper to have prevented soil contamination in the first place, the Dutch now face a bill of eighteen billion euros for the total cleanup of their soil. They will not be able to succeed with the problem by 2023, and the goal has been postponed to 2030. Those who caused the problem, own the soil, or have it on lease will pay for 75 percent of the costs of cleaning up. In 2002 this percentage was met in soil cleanup in cities. Outside of cities, 55 percent of the costs are paid by private parties. Another example of the government's innovative thinking is its agreement with the car manufacturers of Europe. In this agreement, auto manufacturers take responsibility for making sure that their cars are disposed of in ways that will have the least impact on the environment. This is a lifecycle management approach and, as mentioned above, has led to such innovations as Volkswagen's clear marking of plastic car parts for recycling.

The NEPP's target-group approach has in particular yielded some unexpected and very encouraging benefits. For example, the energy distribution target group produced an environmental action plan that achieved 90 percent of its carbon-dioxide reduction-target in its first year and subsequently set for itself even more ambitious goals.[27] A number of other industries have also chosen to set more ambitious targets for themselves than those required by the NEPP.

In some cases, the target-group approach has led to greater cooperation among industries in order to reach environmental goals. One example is the packaging industry, where manufacturers, importers, distributors, and retailers have joined forces to increase their efficiency in achieving the targets required of them.

The Dutch have also encountered setbacks, of course. They were not able to reach their initial goals for carbon-dioxide reductions. Reasons include the greatly reduced price of energy in recent years that has encouraged the number of cars to increase at a greater rate than they had anticipated, and has also allowed people to keep driving less fuel-efficient cars. They are considering imposing a carbon tax, but prefer to do so in conjunction with other members of the European Union. The Netherlands' carbon tax will be bolstered by a new carbon-based tax on packaging, the first of its kind in Europe.

New Zealand

It is fitting that a historically progressive nation such as New Zealand, which was the first country to give women the right to vote, has launched an effective Green Plan.

In 1991, following nearly a decade of economic restructuring along the lines of Reaganomic-Thatcherism, New Zealand enacted a model of environmental policy, a Green Plan, called the Resource Management Act (RMA). The RMA was a remarkable achievement, primarily for three reasons. First, it was based on the desire to maintain a high level of quality of life for the residents of New Zealand. Second, it made major, almost revolutionary, changes in government. The RMA entirely restructured New Zealand's resource agencies and laws around the premise of what they term "sustainable management."[1] Finally the RMA, which was introduced to the public through a broad program of public education, raised the level of public awareness and involvement in the process of reform.

Like the Netherlands, New Zealand has shifted away from precise regulation of how resources are to be used. Instead, they regulate the effects of such use, or how such use will impact the environment. Unlike the Dutch, who, because of the state of their environment, developed a system that focuses on the recovery levels they want to achieve, New Zealand's Plan focuses on the underlying philosophy. With the RMA and its philosophy of sustainable management, New Zealand has developed a carefully thought-out framework for structuring what all its present and future decisions should be regarding resource management, its values, goals, and considerations.

The momentum for New Zealand's Plan came in part from the public's angry reaction to an earlier administration's push for massive development. In the late 1970s and early 1980s the then minister of energy began promoting development in the form of "Think Big" projects, including a series of energy-related projects such as a synthetic gas-to-gasoline plant, a methanol plant, and a major dam on one of New Zealand's wild and scenic rivers. In order to secure his ambitions, this minister passed the National Development Act, which made him the final decision maker on these projects, barring or limiting local governments, courts, and the public from decision-making processes. The public so disliked the proposal that in the next election the more environmentally oriented Labor Party came to power, intent on changing and upgrading New Zealand's environmental laws. The National Development Act was repealed and the movement toward Green Plans got underway.

Geoffrey Palmer, the new deputy prime minister, who later became prime minister, appointed himself as minister of the environment. This dual authority, and a special committee he established comprised of the key ministers of finance, local government, commerce, energy, and transport, gave the government considerably more power to make major environmental reforms. The parliamentary select committee took this process to its third reading (or vote) by parliament and was instrumental in the definition and passage of the RMA. The process took a great deal of time, though, and despite bipartisan support for the RMA in parliament, Palmer and his colleagues were unable to pass it into law before the general election. The dream had to be carried over into the next parliament.

The new, conservative National Party government was initially concerned that the reforms did not represent an adequate balance between the environment and the economy. However, the public and the new prime minister's political backers, including his minister for the environment, were solidly behind the reform process and the held-over bill (RMA), so when he proposed backing off the Plan, the voters howled. Being a wise politician, he went with the voters, and his new government took up the legislation and even made slight improvements before passing it in 1991. This success is significant for political theory.

New Zealand, like Holland, has been exemplary in the way it successfully launched its Green Plans. In Holland, it was industry's leadership that influenced the change to try to work in a better way. In New Zealand, it was forwarded by broad public support created in constant discussions regarding what the legislation should contain. The public in each country had a different traditional role. In the Netherlands, where the government tends to be comfortably oriented from the top down, people elect their officials, trust their decisions, and if they don't work well, throw them out of office. In New Zealand there is far greater ongoing involvement on the part of the voters, including a parliamentary select committee process (similar to our Senate hearings), with sessions also held outside their capital, where people can present their written submissions on proposed legislation.

So with the new government agreeing, the RMA was reintroduced in parliament (reintroduced because, as I said, the previous government had spent so much time trying to perfect the Act that it never made it to a final vote). It passed with flying colors, supported by both liberal and conservative politicians as well as a broad cross-section of the public. Having enjoyed the leadership of both major parties, it will be difficult for a new government to stop the program now, even if it wanted to, although change over time is inevitable. Over the years, as new problems have arisen and new information has been gathered, there have been changes, and there will be more, but the overall purpose of recovering environmental quality is firmly planted and growing stronger in New Zealand society.

NEW ZEALAND'S ENVIRONMENT

New Zealand is an island nation about the size of the state of California and located in the South Pacific Ocean. Many rare plants and animals evolved there in isolation from the larger land masses, including many flightless birds. When the first humans, the Maori, landed in New Zealand about a thousand years ago, approximately 80 percent of the country was forested.

Although the Maori initially burned some areas of the country, causing bird extinctions, when the Europeans arrived about 150 years ago, about two-thirds of the original forest cover remained. Since the arrival of the Europeans, much of the remaining original forest has been cut or burned. The Europeans also turned much of the land to pasture or farming, built towns and roads, and introduced new plants and animals, all of which has had significant impacts on the country's ecosystems.

Most of the population of New Zealand is based in urban centers and while the economy is largely rural, the population's attitudes and lifestyles are primarily urban. At the same time, New Zealand's current major industries—farming, forestry, horticulture, fishing, minerals extraction, and, more recently, tourism—are highly resource dependent.[2]

NEW ZEALAND'S ENVIRONMENTAL PROBLEMS

Fortunately, most of New Zealand's environmental problems have not yet reached the level of many Northern Hemisphere countries. This is due in part to its smaller population, and also to its relative lack of heavy industry. New Zealand has relied on its resource-based economy rather than on heavy industry, trading for the industrial products it needs.

This resource-based economy, instead of an industrial economic base, has led to different types of environmental problems caused by pressures put on the resources. For example, instead of having the air, water, and soil contaminated by waste from mismanaged steel plants, New Zealand's environment has been damaged by poor practices in the farming and forestry industries, and from the introduction of nonindigenous species into its ecosystems. Let's turn to a discussion of some specific areas of environmental concern.

Agriculture

As in other developed nations, unsustainable agriculture has been a problem for New Zealand. Modern agricultural practices such as monoculture and the heavy use of fertilizers, pesticides, machinery, and irrigation have all had a negative impact on the country's soil, water, species diversity, and natural ecosystems. Until recently, New Zealand's main industry was livestock farming, primarily sheep. Sheep monoculture can be very hard on farmland, particularly with New Zealand's emphasis on high levels of production, and especially on marginal farmland with a high risk of erosion. Despite the negative impacts, the government once subsidized the practice of clearing marginal land in order to raise more sheep. The decision in early 1984 to end farm subsidies brought needed changes. It came abruptly and ended nearly twenty years of government support for land, livestock, fertilizer, and credit. Farmers adapted to the change by tightening their belts, laying off workers, discontinuing capital expenditures, and generally scaling back. The result has been that operating expenses fell by about 30 percent from 1984 to 1996, which would seem to indicate increased efficiency.

Soil

Some of New Zealand's most serious problems involve threats to soil, including erosion, loss of fertility, compaction, pollution, flooding, and urban encroachment. About 50 percent of the country's land area shows signs of erosion; of this, approximately half is slightly eroded, the other half moderately to severely eroded. Some of the severe erosion in mountainous regions is due to natural causes.

Forest

Among other values ranging from utilitarian timber to peace of mind, forests represent a key element in the prevention of erosion. Under the Forests Act, instigated in 1949 and amended in 1993, indigenous timber can only be produced from forests, which are managed sustainably and according to the requirements of ecological balance.[3]

Biodiversity

Wildlife and biodiversity are especially significant indicators of New Zealand's environmental quality. New Zealand's indigenous plants and animals are of international importance because many primitive life forms have survived there. However, many of these native species are threatened or endangered, approximately 18 percent of vertebrates and 16 percent of native flowering plants; and the extinction rate is reportedly among the world's highest. In fact, decline in indigenous biodiversity has been called "New Zealand's most pervasive environmental issue" in the state of New Zealand's environmental report. In an attempt to prevent further decline, and in recognition of the importance of New Zealand's unique and varied species to the world, New Zealand launched a Biodiversity Strategy in 2000. This Strategy is designed to help New Zealand conserve its precious species through conservation and sustainable management. New Zealand recognizes that the quality of its natural environment and its wealth of flora and fauna is important to its international reputation and trade opportunity. To New Zealand, preservation of species makes economic as well as aesthetic *sense*.[4]

Fish and Shellfish

Although a valuable resource, fish and shellfish face decline because of overexploitation in the past. Due to inadequate regulatory systems, some types of fish and shellfish have been overexploited and related fisheries are declining. Environmental factors including toxic algae blooms, mystery viruses, bacterial contamination, and various diseases, including the recent "black rot," continue to contribute to the damage of fish, shellfish, and even sea birds, seals, and penguins.[5]

Wetlands

Development has devastated wetlands; and drainage, reclamation, and pollution have taken their toll as well. Waste management practices are another problem for New Zealand. With a small population, volumes of waste have been low, and landfill sites have been chosen for convenience rather than for ecological reasons. It is becoming difficult to find suitable new sites in and around the major urban areas. Currently, the target set by the Ministry of Environment for organic waste reduction is for the diversion of 95 percent of commercial organic wastes from landfill to beneficial use by 2010.[6]

THE POLITICAL BASIS OF THE RESOURCE MANAGEMENT ACT

Political courage is a critical element to an idea like Green Plans, the success of which really provides a political science lesson.

In all three countries, the Netherlands, New Zealand, and Singapore, there were government officials who took a progressive and courageous position in launching these ideas. The process of changing New Zealand's environmental laws began in 1988. Both government and citizens realized that they had been passing laws for a hundred years or more that were overlapping, contradictory, unclear, or riddled with gaps. The laws simply were not accomplishing the purpose of protecting the country's natural resources.

The New Zealand government realized it was pointless to try to reform this tangle of regulations and interventions piece by piece, and so they decided to start over. It initiated a three-phase review process, to be conducted by the government with participation from all segments of society. The phases were: (a) to ask and answer the question of whether there should be a law for the management of natural and physical resources, and which resources should be included; (b) to look at options for achieving the objectives defined in the first phase, and to choose the best means; and (c) to develop specific policies and draft appropriate laws.[7]

The process of public review was remarkably thorough, possibly as thorough as any undertaken by any democratic nation in history. It involved all sectors of the public and took at least three years, leaving no stone unturned. Hundreds of meetings were held throughout the country in all major cities. After the hearings, the field team would go back to the home office and discuss its findings.

To facilitate communication, the government established a toll-free phone number and elicited considerable discussion on television and radio. Altogether, the government received more than five thousand responses from the public. The result was a broad-based consensus on goals and the best means for achieving them. From that consensus came a single, coherent, consistent law, the Resource Management Act, which took effect on October 1, 1991.

New Zealand's form of government itself facilitated its environmental law reform. It has a unicameral legislature; that is, it has only one house. The leader of the majority party becomes prime minister, and the cabinet of twenty or so ministers is also chosen from the majority party. There is no written constitution and no federal system of provinces. The executive can therefore make major changes to laws relatively quickly; this is how the RMA was created.

New Zealand's small, largely homogenous population also made it easier to achieve the kind of consensus needed to enact radical reforms. The government review process discussed above built public support for the RMA, creating a national consensus. Although public education is still needed, most of the population now understands the importance of sustainable management of resources. The government policy is to continue providing as much information as possible to the people, so they will see what the program is accomplishing and what actions are necessary on their part.

Several influential social groups in New Zealand played particularly crucial roles in the creation of its Green Plan, and continue to play equally large roles in its implementation. One of these is the Maori, citizens of Polynesian heritage and the country's first human inhabitants. The Maori were entirely dependent on natural resources and they found they had to adopt sustainable practices in order to survive.[8]

The Maori have been granted rights as indigenous people that are different from the entitlements of other citizens, particularly in terms of resources. For this reason, the management structure of the RMA has a component that deals directly with the Maori as a distinct political constituency. Maoris also have a well-organized tribal structure and their own representatives in the national parliament, and it is the government's intention that tribal authorities be consulted regarding resource management issues. In addition to the existence of a Maori electoral roll and electorates there is now a new political party (the Maori

Party) established in 2004 following the government's moves to curtail Maori claims to the foreshore and seabed. It has one Member of Parliament, formerly a Labor Party MP elected to one of the Maori electorates.

Business groups also played an important role in enacting the RMA and are playing an even larger role in its implementation. As in most countries, New Zealand's business community tends to be conservative, and was initially suspicious of the Act, but from the outset the government included key trade associations of each industry, particularly the primary industries, in the planning process. Far from having the RMA imposed on them, these groups took part in the process of creating it. Since 2000, some business interests, such as the Auckland Chamber of Commerce and Employers and Manufacturers Association, continue to express antagonism to the Plan, while others, such as the New Zealand Business Council for Sustainability, have embraced the concept of sustainability.

Early in the process, I spoke with the representative of a cross-sectional association of forty resource-using companies, who took the most aggressive stance I have heard from a business leader anywhere. He told me that business interests had at first fought the reforms, but realized in the end that they had to make a total commitment; they had to work together to establish a major environmental statement for the nation and really make a difference for the future. They came to realize, he told me, that their old behavior of approaching government from a self-interested perspective had not worked. One timber company would manage to change the rules to its benefit, then a trucking company would come along and have the rules changed again. This manipulation to benefit narrow interests went on to some degree even when companies banded together in trade associations, because they were still operating from a completely self-interested position. Seeing this, the companies in this association decided to do the idealistic thing and support the adoption of sound environmental practices, under which all businesses would be treated the same.

An interesting additional insight from those meetings was, as one of the participants pointed out to me, that while there were participants from a broad sector of New Zealand's industries, there were no real-estate development representatives in these meetings. They had chosen to oppose the Green Plan idea. They didn't like planning. So, as he said, they just kind of booted them out. This is similar to what I've observed in many rural counties in the United States. This is a predominately limiting factor for environmental planning success. It's a condition that has been ignored or not seen; and until industries understand that comprehensive environmental quality allows them greater efficiency, it's unlikely to improve. That means there are always opponents in any free society, attempting to bring about changes in the direction that they favor. In the United States for instance, real-estate development is very powerful, particularly in rural areas—to the detriment of the nation. But that too will change.

One reason that it was relatively easy for the government to get the leaders of trade associations to agree to work with it on resource issues is that New Zealand's economy depends so heavily on natural resources. It was particularly successful in enlisting farmers, who represent New Zealand's largest industry. The farm industry was at the point where it saw the economic advantage in sustainable production, and in some cases it has gone beyond government requirements by setting higher standards of environmental quality.

The Federated Farmers, the farming industry's primary association, came to realize that environmental sustainability was not only the key to survival, but also a great marketing advantage. High-quality meat, dairy, and produce raised without large quantities of fertilizers and pesticides are attractive to many consumers in countries like the United States, particularly if it costs less. New Zealand can produce these foods more cheaply than most countries because it has lower energy inputs for agriculture.

Nonprofit environmental groups also played an important role in drafting the RMA by participating in negotiations throughout the years it took to develop the Act. However, as befits the diverse nonprofit environmental movement today, some of the groups have remained skeptical, playing the role of critics. Compromises have had to be made when creating and implementing a complex law like this, and it has been important to have watchdogs to keep up the pressure for improvements and alert the public to any defects.

Environmental groups have also helped the process along by public education. In New Zealand, the government has a program of environmental grants, which gives funds to environmental groups to establish and maintain educational programs in communities across the country. Tax laws in New Zealand don't give a benefit to the donor when money is given to a nonprofit, as is done in the United States, so they are leaner financially. One observation is that many nonprofit organizations get funding from whatever sources they can, including government. While that has worked well in the Dutch case, in New Zealand there is a problem in that these nonprofits will be competing for grants. In addition, those who will be giving them grants are inside government and inclined to fund organizations for which they have an affinity; and they will tend to fund outfits that are likely to be gentle in their criticism toward them later. The really important critics are not likely seen as suitable. So it isn't foolproof.

THE PHILOSOPHIC BASIS OF THE RESOURCE MANAGEMENT ACT

Two key themes of Green Plans are comprehensiveness and integration. The RMA represents a truly radical break from traditional approaches to environmental planning. At its core are two key philosophical differences. The first, which it shares with the plans of both the Netherlands and Singapore, is the move from a narrow, piecemeal approach to a more comprehensive and integrated view of resource management. The second difference is the concept of sustainable management as the structuring principle behind the country's environmental laws and policies.

In the past, like many other countries, New Zealand approached the management of resources as a technological challenge geared to solving one problem or one need, and would plan, for example, to build levees to stop floods or irrigation systems to supply arid regions. However, like other countries, it found that approach seriously flawed, often causing more problems than it solved.

For instance, they would deal with a flooding problem by looking at only one part of the picture—the area in which the river floods—and then building levees and dams to control it. In the long run, that was more expensive, less effective, and more environmentally damaging than if they had looked at the whole picture and realized that a better answer was to plant trees on the steep, deforested slopes upstream, which would lead to much less water runoff and siltation. Another was to allow flood-plain zoning so that damage to buildings wouldn't occur during overflow periods. Or, taken one step further, if they had identified areas of flood hazard and provided that information to local authorities and the public, better decisions could have been made regarding the proper use for the land.

The RMA has been designed to allow communities and regions to take that broader approach. The comprehensive framework allows for the integration of institutions and systems dealing with resources, so that the environment can be managed as a whole, instead of in an inefficient, piecemeal fashion. Now communities can create long-term, comprehensive management programs for their resources, supported by the enabling legislation of the RMA, and by money and ideas from the government.

New Zealand's push toward comprehensiveness and integration led to a massive restructuring of government as part of the changes that led to the RMA. The RMA replaced fifty-seven existing resource-related laws, and whittled eight hundred units of government (this included a multitude of little water boards and trust boards and so forth) down to ninety-three units of government. It consolidated government into two levels, national and local, then divided local government into regional authorities, which are based on watersheds, and district authorities. Both government and the regulatory process have been streamlined to make them more effective and efficient; the intent of the RMA has been to get the maximum environmental benefit with a minimum of regulation.[9]

As the New Zealanders discovered, these efficiencies could not be achieved without first determining the ultimate goal of their resource policy. During the review process, they identified this goal as the sustainable management of resources and refined the concept through further debate. The definition they finally arrived at is stated in section 5(2) of the RMA as: managing the use, development, and protection of natural and physical resources in a way, or at a rate, which enables people and communities to provide for their social, economic, and cultural well-being and for their health and safety while: (a) sustaining the potential of natural and physical resources (excluding minerals) to meet the reasonably foreseeable needs of future generations; (b) safeguarding the life-supporting capacity of air, water, soil, and ecosystems; and (c) avoiding, remedying, or mitigating any adverse effects of activities on the environment.

All parts of the RMA, and any decisions made and actions taken under it, are required to meet these principles of sustainable management. The Act also recognizes that definitions of sustainability are not static and will change as the store of environmental information grows.

New Zealand's ultimate goal is sustainable development, but the RMA does not attempt to provide that by itself. Sustainable development, as the government's review group concluded, embraces a very wide range of issues including social inequities, global redistribution of wealth, and population density problems. In their discussions they were realistic in saying environmental law can't cover all the legislative needs of the nation. The group found this range too complex for a law designed to manage the natural resources of a single nation. Consequently, their definition of sustainable management does not address the question of development; it is neither anti-nor pro-development. In promoting sustainable management, the government is not as concerned with how the land is used as it is with how various land uses affect the environment and other people. They have shifted from planning for activities to regulating the effects of activities.

The RMA provides a structure within which decisions are made about the way community-owned and -managed resources are allocated, determining who is allowed to use such public resources as water, air, the coastal area, and geothermal energy. It also determines what they may be used for. The Act also applies the principle of sustainable management to privately owned property, setting the standards of environmental quality that private owners must adhere to when making decisions about the use of their own property.

To apply quality-control standards to every public and private decision about land use is a powerful change in thinking about environmental law and resource management. Other countries do this to some extent through permits and regulations, but New Zealand is the first country to codify into law the idea that the government has a right to require private landowners to meet certain standards. The judicial system in the United States is just beginning to deal with this issue.

New Zealand's policy is not a strict code of behavior, however. Rather than telling people how to use their land through controls like zoning, the government gives people standards for environmental quality that must be met regardless of land use. In taking this approach, the government is trying to achieve two almost contradictory goals: first, allowing people the maximum freedom in their use of resources; and second, ensuring that those activities have the minimum adverse affect on environmental sustainability.

Instead of saying, "You will put houses here" and "You will put industry there," the RMA has set up a process for developing standards of environmental quality that will be consistent with sustainability, and which will be specified in fairly clear ways. Within that framework people have the freedom to do what they please. For example, a recent environment court ruled that the public roads authority (Transit NZ) would have to design a new freeway so as not to remove part of a regionally significant dormant volcanic cone in Auckland.

HOW THE RESOURCE MANAGEMENT ACT WORKS

Under the RMA, the national government has two complementary means for expressing and applying its resource management policies: national policy statements and national environmental standards.[10] Policy statements express national goals and objectives for the environment and its sustainable management; they are descriptive rather than prescriptive, and cover issues of resource protection, use, and development. The statements may also deal with general issues, such as New Zealand's obligations in enhancing the global environment, or they may be quite specific about a particular issue or site. The only national policy statement the government is required to develop is the New Zealand Coastal Policy Statement, dealing with national priorities for the management of the country's coastal environment.

Unlike policy statements, national environmental standards are prescriptive, and are promulgated as regulations. They apply to the entire nation; regional and local plans and policies cannot violate them. They set technical standards relating to the use, development, and protection of natural and physical resources, including standards for contaminants; water quality, level, or flow; air quality; and soil quality. Typically these are bottom-line standards, beyond which one cannot go and still practice sustainable management, but they can go further in particular situations.

Regional and district governments have borne the most responsibility for implementing the RMA. The Act restructured regional government into sixteen units based primarily on watersheds and their ecosystems, which are the most logical units upon which to base environmental management. Directly elected regional authorities are responsible for preparing regional policy statements and plans. All regional and district policies and plans must be consistent with and reflect national policy statements and standards, and all must uphold the principle of sustainable management.

Regional policy statements are mandatory, because they articulate the key issues and priorities for each region, interpreting sustainable management and applying it to the region's biophysical and socioeconomic characteristics. They identify key resources and their condition, determine the community's relationship to and dependency on those resources, and identify links among resources and ecosystem issues and problems. Based on those factors and taking into consideration future needs and potential pressures, regional policy statements develop strategies for sustainable resource management and identify priority issues and responses. They are statements of policy only; the regulatory measures required to implement them have been generated separately.

Regional plans are optional, except for coastal plans. They deal with specific resource issues requiring more detailed policies and can provide the regulatory power to implement regional policies. The regional authorities can use plans to deal with such issues as regional land-use effects, soil conservation, water conservation and quality, and pollution discharges.

District government units are based on communities and their surrounding areas, and each one is required to promulgate its own plan. District plans have policies relating to the integrated management of the effects of land use, subdivision, the control of noise emissions, and the effects of activities on the surface of water in rivers and lakes.

Streamlining the permitting process was considered a key element of the Act. If a landowner is not operating, or is not able to operate, within the standards established for water quality, air quality, waste disposal, soil management, and so on, he or she is required to get a special permit, and has to go through a public process involving an assessment of all the effects of the activity. The permit process in most cases is simpler and quicker than it previously was, because now there is only one standard permit process and a standard time limit to that process. Only the local and regional councils will issue permits, rather than a whole host of small boards. If permits are needed from both councils for one property (for example, a factory needs both permission to build at the site and permission to discharge contaminants into a stream), there is only one combined hearing process. The fact that the permit process has been simplified does not mean that it is necessarily easier to *get* a permit; the sustainability of the proposed action is always the bottom line.

MONITORING, ENFORCEMENT, AND APPEALS

Monitoring is an important part of the RMA. Some of the laws replaced by the Act contained no provisions for monitoring, which led to regulation without any real idea of whether or not the regulation was needed or did what it was supposed to do. The RMA requires the gathering of information relating to sustainability and monitoring of the state of the environment. It also requires monitoring of the suitability and effectiveness of any policy statement or plan, and of the use of resource permits that have been granted.

Prior to the RMA, the government had already established a parliamentary commissioner for the environment as an independent auditor to monitor the effectiveness of the country's resource laws and institutions. Since its inception in 1987, the commissioner's office has presented numerous reports to the House of Representatives, to parliamentary committees, and to public authorities. In April 2008, it published its final report on New Zealand's progress.[11]

This type of monitoring is not related to enforcement. Rather, it involves knowing why objectives have been set, when and what ends or results are expected, and also checking to see that the methods chosen to achieve those objectives are still relevant and that the costs of achieving them are still worthwhile. The information gathered from monitoring is required to be made public under the RMA.

There are provisions for enforcement of the Act, and penalties prescribed for violations, as laid out in the Act itself, can be quite severe. Directors of companies that are not in compliance may be liable, and penalties in some cases can even involve jail terms.

The planning tribunals, or environmental courts, are courts of appeals regarding the planning and implementation of the RMA. The environmental courts get involved at two levels. One is the policymaking level: The courts can rule on whether or not a particular plan or policy is in compliance with the requirement to promote sustainable management. The courts have the power to make an independent judgment on what does or does not constitute sustainable management and can go against the judgment of a municipal or regional council.

The other level on which the courts operate is that of permit granting and the enforcement of standards. They can determine whether or not a particular permit was granted in violation of the sustainable management requirement, or denied when it should not have been. The courts have the power to require permit holders to comply with the terms of their permits, or to meet different standards if circumstances change. Even those who have not been required to obtain a permit can fall under the courts' jurisdiction if their actions run contrary to the performance standards set by the relevant plans. Any person can request the courts to take these enforcement actions.

The court consists of a judge and one or more commissioners who are laypersons with warrants issued by the governor-general. Environmental court judges are chosen solely for the purpose of making environmental decisions and are appointed for life, so they have the opportunity to acquire a considerable amount of knowledge about the environment. Consequently, a judge rarely makes environmental decisions on matters he or she knows nothing about. The courts also have members who are not judges, but come from different sectors of society. Environmental court judges also hold district court warrants enabling them to deal with breaches of the Act. Courts are required to explain what is included in their monitoring and how they are to carry out their monitoring in the regional policy statement and the district plan.

PROGRAMS OUTSIDE THE RESOURCE MANAGEMENT ACT

The RMA is the backbone of New Zealand's overall environmental program, designed to structure a large number of decisions, but it is not the *only* part of it. There are special environmental programs that fall outside of the scope of the RMA. Some were created before the RMA and the government wished to continue them; others required a more detailed handling than could be accommodated by the RMA. They include a program on climate change, one on hazardous substances, and another one dealing with waste management. The latter project, which emphasizes minimization of waste and clean technology in particular, is being done principally through cooperation with industry—beginning with the packaging industry.

Legislation covering mining activities was also dealt with outside the RMA, in large part due to the fact that the Crown owns all gold, silver, uranium, and petroleum. Under the new legislation that has been written in this area, the Crown remains responsible for the granting of mining rights to companies, but the environmental effects of that mining now fall under the jurisdiction of the regional and local authorities, which have the authority to grant permits and set conditions.

These programs are all in accordance with the RMA's goal of sustainable management, but while some of the measures used to implement them operate within the RMA framework, others do not. For example, the climate change program might make use of the part of the RMA that deals with standards for air quality, but beyond the RMA standards, the program will have its own targets and will use a variety of additional measures to achieve them. For instance, New Zealand joined other developed countries in accepting the Kyoto Protocol target of maintaining 1990 levels of carbon-dioxide emissions by the year 2000. New Zealand ratified the Protocol in December 2002, and by 2003, New Zealand's emissions began to decrease.[12]

The Department of Conservation was also created independently of the RMA. Its specific responsibilities are to preserve and protect indigenous species and habitat on government land and to advocate their protection on private land. However, the RMA would also come into play if someone wanted to develop land that was important indigenous habitat; because of the Act's provisions, they would probably not be allowed to do so.

PROGRESS TOWARD SUSTAINABILITY

New Zealand, through the RMA and other governmental reforms, has already made some progress toward the idea of sustainable management; the preservation of native forests is one example. At the time the RMA was passed, the government found that 35 percent of New Zealand's original forest was still standing, and that by focusing on intensive tree farming they could afford to put the remaining old growth in permanent preserve status, which they have done. They no longer look at the forest as simply a wood resource, but as an entity that has value of its own. Therefore, the wood that people take from it has to be taken in a way that observes the principles of eco-sustainability, even on private land.

As mentioned above, the farming industry has also made great leaps toward sustainability. One reason is that the country simply stopped subsidizing agriculture. The story of how they did that is fairly dramatic. During a late night parliamentary session in which representatives were debating the country's problems and how to avert impending bankruptcy, someone said, "Cancel agricultural subsidies." So the farmers woke the next morning with no subsidies. That was a fascinating, drastic decision, but it really worked for them. It culled out the marginal operators, and most of the viable farmers adapted comfortably, with the help of government loans to ease their transition. Agriculture is healthier now than it was with subsidies. This action dramatically cut environmental degradation, bringing to an abrupt halt many damaging practices like the application of pesticides and fertilizers. Existing irrigation subsidies were also removed and as a result New Zealand no longer has any new mega-irrigation schemes. Farmers began to realize that they were on their own and could no longer assume the government would save them if they ran into difficulty. They realized their businesses must be better managed, in a way that fits with nature. Also, as mentioned earlier, farmers have found sustainable practices can also be quite profitable. They believe they can do better by specializing rather than by going for a mass market, which has long been the tradition in New Zealand. Now, instead of providing large quantities of lamb and wool to export to England, they are emphasizing quality and targeting discerning consumers who want "clean, green" products.

A transition period of five years was built into preparing the
RMA, to give the government time to develop and implement
the necessary standards, policies, and practices. Most of the
regional policy statements had been released for public com-
ment by the time of the publication of the first edition of this
book, and the Minister of Conservation was reviewing the National Coastal Policy Statement. Other standards and policies
have followed. Regional policy statements have been intended
to have a ten-year life, but their horizon has so far extended up
to twenty years beyond that. At the start, Lindsay Gow, deputy
secretary of New Zealand's Ministry of Environment, described
policies and plans under the RMA as "rolling sustainable management programs, updating issues continuously while having
an ever-extending outer horizon."

According to the above-mentioned report from the parliamentary commissioner for the environment, in the future the
government will need to take action on a number of specific
items in order to move toward sustainable management in all
resource areas. Gaps noted by the commissioner include the
lack of government policies on certain issues involving energy
conservation and energy efficiency, and sewage treatment and
disposal. The government also needs to develop an overall strategy to improve public transit.

Another potential weakness of the RMA has been that it does
not in itself deal with international issues and policies, in contrast to the Netherlands' National Environmental Policy Plan.
One of the reasons for this is context: The Netherlands is surrounded by other nations and so has much more interaction
with them on a regular basis. Their economies are linked, and
their pollution more perceptibly shared. Therefore, the Netherlands has a much more outward perspective than New Zealand,
which is an island six hundred miles removed from any other
country, tending to view itself in isolation.

As of this writing, we are three years from the fulfillment of the "New Zealand 2010" program, instigated in October 1994, and setting the goal for the next step toward sustainability by the year 2010. New Zealand 2010 will fill many of the gaps mentioned above. It is specifically an environmental strategy, whereas most of the government's strategies to date have been principally economic. While the country's focus on the principles of the market economy is designed to meet economic needs, 2010 is designed to establish and maintain environmental quality for future generations.

New Zealand 2010 sets a vision for the future, articulating the values and philosophical principles New Zealanders want to have embodied in their environmental strategies. It also involves the setting of the ecological bottom line, which will establish strict limits to pollution and to the use of natural resources, based on the best scientific and technical information. For example, all forests are to be managed strictly on a sustainable basis; no harvest can exceed the growth rates of the forest. Nonrenewables will be managed carefully, and a major policy thrust will be to seek alternatives to nonrenewables.

As part of the 2010 program, the government will

- weave environmental policy into economic and social policy;
- establish a coherent framework of laws (this will particularly link 2010 to the RMA);
- sharpen the policy tools needed to carry out the program (for instance, market mechanisms will be used, but not emphasized);
- build up the information base regarding environmental quality. This will help establish indicators and determine environmental costs, which will be particularly useful to decision makers and researchers. With this base, a full-cost pricing policy can be implemented,

which will ensure that subsidies do not creep into and manipulate the management of key natural resources;
- involve people in the decision-making process.

New Zealand 2010 also sets nine goals for managing environmental quality, similar to the goals set by the Dutch in their National Environmental Policy Plan. This type of environmental management by long-term objective has become a key aspect of Green Plans. It allows them to manage the entire spectrum of environmental and resource issues, with all their interconnectedness, and yet not become overwhelmed by the complexity. New Zealand's nine goals are:

- Protect biodiversity
- Control pests, weeds, and diseases
- Control pollution and hazardous wastes
- Manage land resources
- Manage water resources
- Establish sustainable fisheries
- Manage the environmental impacts of the energy sector
- Word toward stopping the causes of climate change
- Restore the ozone layer[13]

Finally, 2010 includes a review process that will assess the programs' progress toward their goals. The planning and review process will involve a five-year cycle and a one-year cycle, and a report to the people every four years.

Unlike such industrialized nations as the Netherlands, New Zealand has the luxury of focusing more on the management of resources than on cleaning up pollution. As a result, it has been able to come up with the better philosophical framework of resource management. From my perspective, the important thing for New Zealand is that they understand the importance of its accomplishment with this program and create a global outreach making their ideas available to other nations.

Many of the developing nations tend to see development

only as technical and industrial growth, but the New Zealand example of harnessing systems to produce economic returns while maintaining strong environmental quality standards may be far more effective from a number of standpoints, particularly when a nation does not have the resources for heavy manufacturing.

A strength of New Zealand's program is that the framework of the RMA was designed not just to affect the way government operates but also the actions of every citizen, so that all the decisions people make respecting the land, water, air, or coast fit within its framework. Another strength of the RMA is its coordination of objectives. Sustainable management of resources is the primary drive within every framework, whether it is economic growth or something else. One is part of the other, but, as Lindsay Gow says, "The environment is the top line and the bottom line."

CHAPTER SEVEN

Toward a Sustainable Singapore

We do not allow the lack of natural endowment to determine our fate. Instead, we look ahead, plan for the future,
set clear targets, and pursue the necessary policies head
on with clear thinking and concrete strategies. However,
the successful implementation of SGP2012 will not happen overnight. All of us must be prepared to play our
part, and commit ourselves to act in a timely and responsive way. —*Lim Swee Say*

Singapore, a city-state characterized in the last few decades by
rapid industrial growth and essentially no natural resources,
may seem like an unlikely candidate for Green Planning.[1] Yet
it may have been precisely the limitations of its small, highly
developed land area, aided by its highly centralized government
in which all the departments work in concert, that prompted
Singapore to adopt, in 1992, a comprehensive environmental
program, the Singapore Green Plan (SGP2012).

The country's space limitations have forced it to practice careful land-use planning for many years. For example, since the city's master plan was drawn up in the 1950s, all land has been zoned, and environmental impact assessments have been required for all new development. By the time the 1992 Green Plan was drawn up, Singapore was already known for having some of the world's strictest pollution control standards, including particularly impressive air-quality standards and a modern, congestion-free, and cheap mass transit system. At this writing, some fifteen years into the Plan, Singapore is proud to be successfully achieving economic and social growth while not neglecting the environment. Although a small country, it is one of Asia's leaders in environmental technologies and services.

WHY IS THE SINGAPORE GREEN PLAN WORKING SO WELL?

The Singapore government works closely with business, especially when dealing with environmental issues. When Singapore began to industrialize in the late 1960s, the government decided it wanted to avoid the pollution problems other countries had faced. It focused on preventing them at the source and applied strict regulations from the beginning. As the country developed, it was able to take advantage of new environmental technologies, both in its industries and in the creation of its infrastructure.

In 1992, Singapore issued the Singapore Green Plan (SGP2012) as a preliminary step toward a formal, comprehensive plan. Primarily a vision statement, the Plan listed broad goals in areas across the resource spectrum, and designed a program of environmental education and information aimed at helping citizens and businesses make better environmental decisions.

Although the Plan laid out some specific targets, such as setting aside or reclaiming 5 percent of the country's land as open space and setting more strict emissions standards, it was by nature a more general document, outlining broad strategies to make Singapore a "model green city" by the year 2000.

In response to new challenges, a review was initiated in 1999 and suggestions were made through a National Preparatory Process. This Process included gathering input from stakeholders in all segments of the population, both in the private and public sectors. The result in 2002 was the Singapore Green Plan 2012 (SGP2012), a "roadmap" to lead the country to environmental sustainability by 2012. The "theme" of the plan was: Toward an Enduring Singapore. The Singapore Green Plan 2012 was then presented at the Johannesburg World Summit on Sustainable Development in 2002.

The Singapore Green Plan 2012 is reviewed every three years for feedback and to address current issues. It has three main aims: (1) to ensure a quality living environment through the innovative and efficient use of scarce resources; (2) to promote the active participation of all sectors of the population to sustain a quality living environment; (3) to do their part for the global environment, because environmental degradation knows no boundary. The first review led to a revised SGP2012 in 2006 enabling Singapore to address particulate matter and bring climate change to national attention.

The SGP2012 is carried out by six action program committees (APCs) composed of representatives from government, industry, and the public sector. The APCs each oversee a particular functional area: clean air and climate change, clean water, waste management, conserving nature, public health, and international environmental relations. Within these six functional areas are 155 action programs. Regular monitoring and assessment is performed by the SGP2012 Coordinating Committee and the APCs to keep the efforts on track. Singapore has moved away from government-led campaigns to a more collaborative approach. The community partnership among the 3P's—people, private, and public sectors—works to keep the nation environmentally aware and responsible.[2] Also, NGOs such as the

Singapore Environment Council, Nature Society (Singapore), the Waterways Watch Society, and the Habitat Forum also act as watchdogs. The government acts as a network facilitator, connecting employers, employees, civic groups, labor unions, educators, and media to strengthen the message of environmental sustainability.

WHAT IMPROVEMENTS HAVE BEEN MADE SINCE 1992?

The original Green Plan did not include the integration of environmental concerns throughout government departments and agencies, most likely because integration is the rule rather than the exception for Singapore's highly centralized government, nor did it focus on the development of new strategies for working with business on pollution prevention. It did, however, discuss the idea of the government taking a more proactive role in environmental management by promoting environmental audits and the use of clean technology. Energy conservation, while not covered in the original Green Plan document, is now an important component of the program.

Possibly the weakest part of the original Green Plan was its lack of a strong commitment to natural ecosystems and the conservation of native plants and wildlife. The current Plan seeks to "strike a pragmatic balance" between the inevitable and growing needs of development and preservation of the "natural heritage."[3] Part of that approach includes documenting indigenous plants and animals, promoting public awareness, and setting land aside for nature reserves, parks, and park connectors. In 2001, in addition to the established Bukit Timah and Central Catchment Nature Reserves and the primary forest in the Singapore Botanic Garden, two new areas, notable for their mangroves and coastal ecosystems were added as nature preserves. This is the first time in its history that the Singapore government has afforded legal protection to an area for nature conservation.[4] In terms of biodiversity, the Singapore National Parks Board, along with the Scientific Authority on Nature Conservation in Singapore, has been undertaking a project monitoring flora and fauna. The results have been encouraging, adding ten additional mammals to Singapore's checklist and including the rediscovery of thirteen species.[5]

Despite these encouraging signs, Singapore is urbanizing rapidly and much of its environment has already been altered. As with other aspects of the Green Plan, "amicable and cooperative partnership between government agencies, nongovernmental organizations, tertiary institutions, private organizations, and dedicated individuals is pivotal to the success of the nature conservation efforts." A key word here is *balance*. Like Holland, as Singapore experiences increasing population growth, with the attendant need for housing and industry, the demands on its limited amount of land will be great. In the 2012 Plan, they resolve to hold on to the land by creative multifaceted usage, such as placing train and bus stations over each other and locating storm-water collection ponds under road flyovers, in addition to building stack factories, underground facilities, and high-rise housing.

SINGAPORE: SMALL, BUT A MODEL FOR GIANTS

Singapore's environmentalism is intended by its government to be a model for developing countries. The UN has cited it as such, not only for its policies and plans, but also for the Environment Ministry's ability to effectively monitor and enforce those policies.

For example, according to a 2003 joint World Bank and Asian Development Bank study of twenty Asian countries, only Singapore's air quality fell within the safety limits for key pollutants.[6] Researchers noted that Singapore has clean air because of strict pollution controls, such as restricting the number of automobiles on the road. The number of automobiles, a key polluter, is growing alarmingly, especially in India and China, where air pollution is growing worse each year. In India, ten thousand new cars move onto the roads each year. In China, car sales have been doubling each year.[7] As a Singapore environment minister reminded me, enforcement of existing laws alone will not be sufficient to maintain good air quality. Cleaner sources of energy and technology and modes of transportation must be explored.

To that end, Singapore's SGP2012 set up the National Energy Efficiency Committee in 2001 to develop programs to encourage more efficient energy use by industries, homes, commercial buildings, and vehicles. The programs include labeling of appliances to inform consumers which ones are energy efficient.[8] They encourage the use of compressed natural gas (CNG), which burns cleaner than diesel. In 2002, the first CNG refueling station in Singapore opened, and at the same time, CNG-powered public busses and taxis were launched. Industries and power stations also are switching to compressed natural gas.[9]

To a tiny, coastal land like Singapore, water is an ever-present concern. Currently, about half the landmass of Singapore is now set aside for water catchment, and that area is set to increase. Through the Four Taps Strategy, Singapore is also studying means of acquiring water from unconventional sources and opened their first desalination plant in 2005. Four plants provide forty-two million gallons per day of NEWater from recycled effluent through advanced membrane technology, while exceeding drinking-water standards by both the World Health Organization and the U.S. Environmental Protection Agency. By 2012, it is planned that 15 percent of all water consumption in Singapore will be NEWater.[10] Improved sewerage is also part of the Plan.

Waste management is another important aspect of the SGP2012, and the ten-year goal is for "zero landfill." Early on in the Plan, approximately 40 percent of the country's paper and cardboard waste flow was being collected for recycling.

The government has now set a target of recycling 60 percent of all waste by the year 2012, reducing the need for new incineration plants from the current rate of one every five to seven years to one every ten to fifteen years. Commercial applications for recycled products are being developed to help make the program viable.[11]

Singapore has also developed excellent information-management systems as one of the key elements of a successful Green Plan. Like the Netherlands, it uses these systems to identify sources of pollution and other environmental problems.

Thanks to its Green Plan, Singapore has found that good environment leads to good health. As a result of environmental improvement, the population of Singapore is enjoying a reduced incidence of tropical diseases and reduced infant mortality, as well as extended life expectancy.

SINGAPORE: A PERSONAL NOTE

When I wrote the section that pertains to Singapore in the first edition of *Green Plans*, I had not been to that country in several years, and so had not had the opportunity to observe in person the amazing transformation Singapore's Green Plan has brought about for its citizens. Even in 1995, I saw a city-state that had been transformed into an impressive, environmentally sparkling, model Green Plan nation. Singapore's impressive economic advances have been matched by its commitment to environmental sustainability, public health, and overall quality of life. It provides an excellent example for other major cities around the world, many of which share the same problems that Singapore understands well—population density, air and water pollution, problems of waste disposal, public health issues, and the need for efficient transit, among others. Like Singapore, these cities will find that a Green Plan can help them revitalize a decaying environmental base.

The success of Singapore's Green Plan is due in part to the

fact that Lee Kuan Yew, the country's first prime minister, who held office from 1959 through 1990, was committed to the environment from the early days of his administration. His environmental efforts began back in the 1960s when he realized that if Malaysia became deforested, it would cost Singapore in lack of rain. So to counteract drought, he began planting trees. He also instigated a "Keep Singapore Clean" campaign, which fined people for littering or spitting. Not only did he clean up the streets, he tackled the two rivers that flow through Singapore, which were both stinking with pollution when he took office. Today, people water-ski on the rivers and fish have returned. Prime Minister Yew was happy with this success and wanted the birds to return also. He consulted the World Wide Fund for Nature to advise him on planting trees and flowers to attract birds. Now, one area of the country is a bird sanctuary. His leadership, not only in building the country, but in instilling an environmental consciousness, has brought his country from an impoverished, environmentally stressed nation to an industrialized power whose citizens enjoy a very high standard of living with high environmental quality.[12]

GREEN PLANS MOVE THE COUNTRY FORWARD

Singapore's environmental regulations set tough standards and are strictly enforced. For example, heads of corporations are held responsible for environmental violations. If a problem occurs, a letter of warning is sent to the executive; if the problem is not corrected, the second letter of warning carries with it a stiff penalty.

Singapore has set some impressive long-term goals for itself, and I believe it will achieve them. A small, tightly knit nation, it may well be managing the problems of population density better than any other area in the world.

CHAPTER
EIGHT | European Union
Environmental Policy

Since my last edition, a major change in the world has been the advance of the European Union. The EU represents a remarkable success story, and part of that story is that its environmental policy is steadily progressing. This was accomplished by its move to an integrated, target-oriented, progressive environmental management plan. The EU has demonstrated that you can balance environmental care with economic concerns through modern regulation and an integrated approach, in dialogue with stakeholders, and by assessing the costs of inaction and the impacts of action in a balanced way.

From an economic perspective that is important to U.S. citizens, another proof of the EU's success is the status of the euro, its new monetary unit. In a world-trade setting, this has impacted the billfold of every family in the United States, whether or not they travel to Europe. Five years ago, if you purchased an item in Europe, say a hat, marked ten euros, its real cost to you in dollars would have been eight dollars. Today, if you buy the same hat, marked ten euros, its real cost in dollars will be twelve dollars.

The example of the EU is dramatic and far advanced beyond anything going on at the federal or state levels in the United States. That is not to say that the states working on a Green Plan haven't benefited. For instance, Oregon, Minnesota, and New Jersey have all benefited by their efforts; however, without a federal policy to support their efforts, achieving success will be far more difficult. Their plans have not resulted in the kind of comprehensive, overall policy that the Green Plans are all about.

WHAT IS THE EUROPEAN UNION AND WHAT IS IT DOING?

The European Union comprises twenty-seven independent nations organized around a common desire for their economic, environmental, and political good. I see the EU as the miracle of the twentieth century, and a worthy alternative to the idea of solving conflicts by war. The most tempting political argument for the EU is that despite the residual anger from generations of war and conflict, the individual countries have been able to unite and successfully work together, even forming a shared currency, the euro. The fact that the euro is becoming strong in competition with the dollar is a measure of the EU's success.

BACKGROUND

As part of the Amsterdam Treaty of 1992, sustainable development was introduced as a key goal for the European Union nations.[1] It required balance between economic, environmental, and other dimensions of policy and is a clear reflection of the goals of sustainable development as discussed in chapter 2.

Although there are conflicts yet unresolved, in comparison with the United States, the EU is about a century ahead in environmental planning and policy. Along with its efforts toward managing environmental quality comes the development of an associated skill in managing other related affairs. For instance, the management of energy has involved developing a careful shared policy on what are the best ways and means of utilizing energy and controlling accompanying problems such as air pollution. The EU is aware of the costs and consequences of industrial processes and is managing them by using the most efficient technology.

ECONOMIC COOPERATION AS THE BASIS FOR POLITICAL COOPERATION

The determining factor in the EU's structure is its reliance on economic partnership rather than a government of states. There is a central governing body and many hope that it will become a nation of states. However, as mentioned earlier, in the election of early 2005 a proposed EU constitution that would have moved the EU more toward a nation of states, comparable to the United States, was defeated through opposition by France and Holland. Despite the failure to create an acceptable constitution, the EU is thriving. The EU model clearly includes heightened attention to the social and ecological dimension. Difficult as it may be to keep social and ecological concerns on the agenda, the EU succeeds in showing that progressive environmental policy is possible without negatively affecting the economy. Clear examples of this are their climate change policy, chemicals policy, and so-called thematic strategies, which I will discuss later in this chapter.

WHY SHOULD WE IN THE UNITED STATES CARE ABOUT THE SUCCESS OF THE EUROPEAN UNION?

The EU comprises twenty-seven independent nations and a population of almost five hundred million people—nearly twice the U.S. population. They can't be ignored, nor can they be pressured, as they are demonstrating already with their requirements on U.S. imports. In addition, when the United States does move toward a comprehensive environmental policy and management plan, the Dutch and EU experience will provide some tested concepts. As I repeat throughout this book, we can learn from their examples. First, the costs of *not* taking action are high, both in real terms and relative to the costs of not taking action; and, second, it pays to tackle problems in an integrated way. Shifting into a comprehensive environmental policy and management plan takes leadership, and knowing that it has already been done successfully by a larger constituency than the United States should inspire us into action.

EUROPEAN UNION DEVELOPMENT: AN HISTORICAL PERSPECTIVE

After World War II, Europe sat in ruins and dreaded any further conflict or destruction such as they had recently experienced. The German Marshall Plan asked European leaders to change the cycle of war that had held Europe in its grip for generations. They decided that the problem, and therefore the solution, was economic. The United States offered $20 million for postwar relief, conditional on the ability of the European countries to join together and draw up a cooperative plan. The thought was that combining their strengths, instead of competing against each other, would ease the rationale for further wars.

The first fifteen EU member nations established an environmental quality standard that remains applicable to all new incoming members. Their system is so appealing that some states in the United States have expressed an interest in joining the EU emissions trading scheme.[2] Whether that is legally possible or not and whether it will actually happen over the coming years is not what is most important now. What is most important is that there is an interest in applying some of the lessons learned from Europe and the EU.

HOW THE EUROPEAN UNION APPROACH WORKS

The EU looks at environmental issues comprehensively by developing policies to manage and solve a number of environmental problems at the same time. The logic is that, by their nature, resource issues are related. For example, burning fossil fuels for transportation or energy use causes air and water pollution. When the quality of air and water is damaged, fish and other aquatic life become dangerous for human consumption, and crop and forest growth becomes compromised. This cascading effect causes resource and health problems. Therefore, the EU has launched seven thematic strategies on soil, marine environment, natural resources, urban environment, pesticides, waste, and air quality.[3] I will be discussing them later in this chapter.

Most nations, including the United States, look at one environmental factor at a time—for example, water quality—and try to correct that, while leaving the rest, such as air quality or wildlife management, for another year, never dealing with the environment as an interrelated whole. Instead of managing to solve *all* of the problem, which is what managing the environment is about, we continue in a old-time horse-and-buggy approach of tackling issues one at a time. By using this piecemeal approach we will not solve the problem of the whole, because there is always a part coming unraveled. There are too many interconnected cause-and-effect relationships for approaches to succeed that deal with only a portion of the problem at any one time.

COMPETITIVE ADVANTAGES OF PROGRESSIVE ENVIRONMENTAL POLICY

The current U.S. president, George W. Bush, and his administration believe that corporations will be saving money if they don't have to include environmental quality–management factors in their operating costs. Unfortunately, that doesn't work in the modern world. Such an approach, which clearly sacrifices environmental concerns, is currently placing stress on the relationship between the United States and the EU. At this time the EU is refusing to import U.S. beef into Europe except that which has been raised without hormones. They specifically reject growth hormones. Recently, the EU has informed U.S. manufacturers that goods containing pollutants like heavy metals will also not be accepted into Europe. These and other examples will hamper U.S. trade. By not living up to environmental standards, the United States may seem to experience an economic competitive advantage, but this will be short term, and will ultimately undermine credibility and future markets for U.S. companies.

It is not only from the short-sighted view that low costs are a misconception. Europeans clearly understand the consequences and costs of inaction. For example, health damage due to exposure of chemicals and fine particulates from traffic is long term and costly. Cleaning soils of toxic residues is a difficult, costly and long-term process. Flooding and soil erosion caused by deforestation and other irresponsible environmental practices also illustrate the high cost of environmental irresponsibility. Neglecting the environment is like creating a short-term wind-fall profit, but, in time, the bill will come and it will be unnecessarily high.

Sadly, rather than learning from the success of the EU, the current U.S. attitude is to attempt to pressure the EU into lowering its standards—an attitude that sets an unfortunate example for the rest of the world. The loudest voice from the United States is the Chamber of Commerce, which maintains a large lobbying effort in the EU headquarters city of Brussels, where it actually works to limit the success of the EU environmental management example. The EU is too large and dedicated to succumb to the pressure from the current U.S. administration and U.S. Chamber of Commerce. Furthermore, it has resulted in anger toward the United States for our meddling in progressive European affairs.

A visit to the Web site of the European Environment Agency (EEA) will give you an overview of recent accomplishments of the European Union's environmental policy, as it monitors a set of around forty environmental indicators.[4] Based on those indicators, it is clear that, among other things, emissions of acidifying gases have decreased significantly in most EEA member countries.[5] Between 1990 and 2002, emissions decreased by 43 percent in the EU-15 and by 58 percent in the EU-10, despite increased economic activity (gross domestic product). Total EU-15 emissions of fine particles were reduced by 39 percent between 1990 and 2002. This was due mainly to reduction in emissions of the secondary particulate precursors, and also to reductions in primary PM-10 emissions from energy industries. In 2002 the greenhouse gas emission was almost 3 percent below 1990 levels. As the EU Kyoto Protocol target is –8 percent, further emission reductions are needed.[6]

In some areas there are clear successes such as the absolute decrease in a number of pressures on the environment, such as nitrous oxide and sulfur dioxide. In other cases, pressures remain high despite the overall increase of the eco-efficiency of economic growth. Local air quality, loss of biodiversity, and climate change remain persistent problems. Efforts to tackle these problems continue and are necessary if the problems in the EU are to be brought under control.

THE EU APPROACH: WHAT IS THE BASIS FOR ITS SUCCESS?

The European Union does not have a Green Plan duplicating the Dutch Green Plan, but it is a comprehensive plan, taking in more than one issue at a time. The cornerstone of EU environmental action is an action program entitled "Environment 2010:

Our Future, Our Choice," covering the period 2001 to 2010. This program addresses four priority issues: climate change and global warming, protecting the natural habitat and wildlife, addressing environment and health issues, and preserving natural resources and managing waste. In addition, the action program emphasizes the importance of enforcing existing environmental laws, considering the environment in all EU policies and maintaining business and consumer involvement. It also emphasizes informing the public about environmental choices, raising awareness of the importance of preserving natural habitats and landscape, and minimizing urban pollution.

So far, the environmental management program of the EU has succeeded. During the life of this and five earlier action programs and after thirty years of standard-setting, the EU has established a comprehensive system of environmental protection. This covers issues of many kinds—from noise to waste, from conservation of the natural habitat to car exhaust fumes, from chemicals to industrial accidents, from bathing water to an EU-wide emergency information and help network to deal with environmental disasters, such as oil spills or forest fires.

The 1993 Treaty of the European Union (TEU) marked a turning point in the European integration process. While stating that Union policy should contribute to the pursuit of preserving, protecting, and improving the quality of the environment, it left room for national action, allowing member states to take even tougher measures than those agreed upon at Union level.

The treaty furthered progress on several fronts. First, it added the concept of "sustainable growth respecting the environment" to the European community's tasks and wrote the precautionary principle into the article on which environmental policy is founded.[7] The treaty required Union policy to aim at a high level of environmental protection, to rectify environmental damage at its source, to be based on taking preventive action, and to make the polluter pay.

The EU strategy for environment and health builds on the recognition that letting conditions decline to the point where they foster ill health is far more costly than maintaining a healthy level of environmental quality. The strategy aims to reduce substantially environment-related health problems, since on a global scale almost 30 percent of diseases can be linked to environmental pressure such as noise, radiation, and substances. The strategy features an integrated approach rather than a fragmented approach and concentrates on specific compartments, like soil, air, and water, at the heart of the program. It focuses on four priority health problems: respiratory health diseases, neurological disorders, cancer, and endocrine disrupting effects. The strategy is elaborated in action plans. The first action plan for 2004–2010 has recently been reviewed.[8]

There are seven thematic strategies in place for soil protection, protection and conservation of the marine environment, sustainable use of pesticides, air pollution, urban environment, sustainable use and management of resources, and waste recycling. These seven thematic strategies are developed according to a common approach independent of their specific subject matter. All the strategies are presented in two stages. In stage one, the existing situation is evaluated and all facts and figures are collected with the cooperation of stakeholders. This is to ensure that proposals are solid and have the scientific, technical, economic, and social backup to overcome counterarguments. In stage two, objectives and targets are defined together with a set of proposals that will contribute to solving the problems. This set of proposals includes precise measures, accompanied by their objectives and timetables, and are capable of implementation.

STRIKING THE BALANCE

Success so far does not mean that there is no pressure on environmental policy. Strong arguments are being made for the need to be less ambitious with future policies for reasons of competitiveness. Strong arguments are also being made to counter this suggestion, as well. Recognizing the pressures on environmental policy, the Dutch launched their "Clean, Clever, Competitive" approach. It aimed to demonstrate that eco-efficient innovations can contribute to growth and competitiveness.

Similar messages come from the European Environment Agency. Based on ongoing research, Jacqueline MacGlade, executive director of the European Environment Agency, put it this way: "We should not accept the fuzzy logic that better regulation equates with less regulation which then leads to lower costs, more competitiveness, and hence more jobs. On the contrary, good regulation can now be shown to reduce costs for industry and business, create new markets, and drive innovation."[9]

For the post-2012 period under debate, arguments have been made to focus on the effects of regulation on the administrative burden for business and how it impacts competitiveness. Environmental concerns will remain a clear part of the integrated assessment after the Kyoto protocol expires. The EU environment ministers successfully argued that the costs of not taking timely action should be taken into account. The heads of the European Environment Agency assessed the contribution of good environmental regulation to competitiveness. They concluded that "modern regulation" can reduce costs for industry and business and help create markets for goods and services as well as drive innovation, reduce business risk, increase investment confidence, and help create and sustain jobs. It also will improve the health of the workforce and the wider public.

The EU is not just talking, but is actually pressing ahead with policy and daring to be ambitious. The formulation of initial ambitions for carbon-dioxide reductions for the period after 2012 is one example. In the original proposal by the European Commission, targets for the period beyond 2012 were absent. There was a loud call from business to take a very close look at the possible effects on competitiveness. Based on cost-benefit analysis of potential reductions, environment ministers agreed to ambitious reduction targets: 15–30 percent reduction of greenhouse gas (GHG) emissions by 2020 and 60–80 percent by 2050.[10]

These goals show that the EU had the courage to take a long-range approach regarding their post-Kyoto ambitions, while we in the United States still deny the necessity of even taking the first steps. They recognized the impact of climate change and acknowledged that in view of the global emission reductions required, global joint efforts are needed in the coming decades.

COST-EFFECTIVENESS OF POLICY

The underlying philosophy of EU policy is changing. Regulation has long been the key instrument of policy leading to cleaner production, cleaner cars, improved recycling, and increasing use of renewable energy. Yet there is a trend toward enhancing more nonlegislative modes of governance and simplifying EU laws. With new regulation, a gradual change seems to be developing toward more focus on target setting and economic instruments. The recently established emissions trading plan for carbon dioxide is a good example.

To combat global warming, all EU member state governments have capped their industries' emissions of carbon dioxide. Companies exceeding their cap must acquire an allowance from companies whose success at emissions reduction has left them with some to spare. These transactions are carried out within the EU's innovative Emissions Trading Scheme (ETS). The ETS is the first international trading system for carbon-dioxide emissions in the world. It covers some twelve thousand installations representing close to half of Europe's emissions of carbon dioxide. Emissions trading does not imply new environmental targets, but aims to achieve national commitments under the Kyoto Protocol in a more cost-effective way. Allowing companies to buy or sell emission allowances means that the targets can be achieved at lowest cost.

In the so-called National Allocation Plans, member states of the EU have allowances they grant to each plant covered by the Emissions Trading Scheme.[11] After the granting, allowances can then be bought or sold by companies among themselves. The European Commission is currently assessing the National Allocation Plans. This assessment and approval of these plans is to ensure that the proposed total quantity of allowances must be in line with a member state's Kyoto target. It must also ensure that the granting of allowances is not a form of state aid leading to discrimination between companies and disruption of a level playing field for competition.

CHEMICALS POLICY

The effect of chemicals on environmental health has become a specter threatening human and environmental health worldwide and may be the most difficult of any of the environmental challenges humanity faces. Long-term use without understanding the dangers has made it possible for chemical pollutants to accumulate in our soils, our drinking water, our air, in living organisms, and ourselves. For instance there is a presence of unhealthy amounts of synthetic chemicals in the breast milk of Eskimos living above the Arctic Circle. This is occurring even though the Eskimo people are thousands of miles away from any manufacturing source. Solving the problem of chemical pollution is a major necessity of our time.

Accepting this as a global challenge, the EU is attempting a dramatic improvement in the use of chemicals. While it is a pioneering effort with a slow start, a characteristic of the EU and emerging policy is persistence, which in the end has a record of making impossible dreams come true.

The program is called REACH (Registration, Evaluation, Authorization, and Restriction of Chemicals).[12] The two most important aims are to improve protection of human health and the environment from the hazards of chemicals, and to enhance the competitiveness of the EU chemicals industry. The approach will attempt to replace sixty old regulations on chemicals. This new policy has been introduced because of a strong feeling that the old policy failed to produce sufficient information about the effects of these chemicals and their risk to human health and the environment. Where risks were identified, the old approach was slow to assess them. The old approach has also hampered research and innovation, causing the EU chemicals industry to lag behind its counterparts in the United States and Japan.

REACH aims to make chemical regulation in Europe more consistent, with improved implementation and less red tape for business. It is a remarkable change giving greater responsibility to industry to manage the risks from chemicals and to provide safety information on substances. Manufacturers and importers will be required to gather information on the properties in their substances, which will help them be managed safely, and to register the information in a central database. A chemicals agency will act as the central point in the REACH system. It will run the databases necessary to operate the system, coordinate the in-depth evaluation of suspicious chemicals, and run a public database in which consumers and professionals can find hazard information.

The ambition and design of the REACH proposal has long been debated. Europe is one of the largest chemical-producing regions, and there was a strong fear that the new REACH policy would negatively affect competitiveness of European businesses. To respond to the concerns of business, the European Commission undertook an impact assessment of the REACH proposal. Its findings are very clear. The overall cost to the chemicals industry and its downstream users would be 2.8 to 5.2 billion euros.[13] From a macroeconomic perspective, the overall impact in terms of the reduction in the EU's gross domestic product is expected to be very limited. The anticipated benefits to environment and human health are expected to be significant.

And there are more benefits. The European chemicals industry will benefit from a single EU regulatory system, decision making with set deadlines, and a high quality image for their products. Users of chemicals will get relevant information on the safe use of each chemical substance they buy. They will have closer contacts with their suppliers, and will be able to ensure better protection of their workers. Their products will be safer for consumers and the environment.

One effect of REACH was to challenge U.S. industry, which exports chemicals to Europe. Another EU directive, the Restriction of Hazardous Substances, has been met by the Silicon Valley electronic communication industry with a positive response. After being told that under the new EU directive they couldn't export computers containing dangerous metals into European Union countries, certain U.S. industries agreed to manufacture their equipment in accordance with EU standards.

This is a much different response than the beef export industry initially gave when it was confronted with an EU challenge to the amounts of hormones and other growth chemicals in U.S. cattle. The U.S. industry has continued to have difficulty exporting beef to Europe.

Since the REACH policy is so substantial, European Union business has taken a very high interest in the design of the policy. As a result, a further impact assessment has been carried out. The environment commissioner concluded that the results show the impacts of REACH to be positive and manageable and that work should continue to help companies readjust to the new standards. Following much discussion, the new EU law on REACH was enacted in June 2007.

The European Union program, which I've described here in brief, and which is amply available on the Web for you to study, is exemplary. The United States, by comparison, is plan-less. With its total emphasis on economic matters, Congress has succeeded in blocking any sense of government planning that would compare with the European Union's program. If twenty-seven separate nations can come together to form cohesive policies, then surely the United States, as well as individual U.S. states, can move ahead and develop a successful and comprehensive Green Plan.

Afterword to the Third Edition

Having observed the progress in the Green Plan countries for nearly twenty years, and having reported my findings in three editions of this book, it is clear to me that the approach works. I believe history will look back and see the success of the European Union and the Green Plan countries as an important transition point in this era of worldwide change.

History will also show that an unexpected benefit of this merger of economy and the environment—which had to be linked together in order for genuine sustainability to succeed—will be that the merger has given life to the concept of sustainability.

This new perspective has serious implications for the United States. Since World War II we have been able to impose upon the world our view that economic prosperity is the dominant issue. Our habit of ignoring the environment has blinded us to the emerging power of sustainability.

But the world has been evolving, and in our belief that we could keep the old way going, we have failed to keep pace. When the Green Plan nations, particularly the EU nations, began to see the need to balance environment and economic development, we resisted; refusing, for example, to join the rest of the world in signing the Kyoto Treaty. In the United States, the fossil fuel industry still enjoys a huge influence in the current political scene—so much so that when the president selected an ambassador to the European Union, he selected a former coal industry spokesperson and lobbyist to promote the president's position.[1]

Nevertheless, despite our objections, the EU countries are moving ahead with sustainable policies. Germany, for example, has created a policy of total solar energy for the future. The government will pay for part of all appliances, and every house and building is considered a power site. Further, Germany has stated that coal and nuclear energy are poisons; their solar program is underway and will replace them as a resource.

While we now lag behind the rest of the world, the United States will scramble, I believe, in the near future. A demonstration of our beginning to move is that a growing number of United States corporations—General Electric, PG&E, Bank of America, Hewlett Packard, Patagonia and others—are seeing the benefits of comprehensive management and are becoming Green—and comfortable with EU standards.

I have every reason to believe that the United States will wake up, join, and ultimately become a leader in this new sustainable world. We have what we need to go forward; we do not need to reinvent the wheel. The path toward restoring and maintaining a healthful quality of life is in place and the rest of the world waits, hoping we will take it. Of course, the reality is that the world is complex. The forces opposing change, especially the fossil fuel interests, are powerful and will attempt to maintain their way of domination. One thing I can predict with confidence is that change will steer us in some unexpected directions.

So much has happened in the last decade that this book could have been several thousand pages long. However, important information is now constantly being updated and made available on Internet Web sites. I suggest, as a way of beginning, that readers visit our Web site at the Resource Renewal Institute at http:/www.rri.org. From there you will be directed to "Green Plans in Action" and other Green Plan sites as well. Web sites of the Green Plan Countries are as follows.

European Union:
European Commission—Environment
http://ec.europa.eu/environment/index_en.htm

The Netherlands:
The Ministry of Housing, Spatial Planning, and the Environment (VROM)
http://international.vrom.nl/pagina.html?id=5450

New Zealand:
New Zealand Ministry for the Environment
http://www.mfe.govt.nz

Singapore:
Ministry of the Environment and Water Resources (MEWR)
http://www.mewr.gov.sg

Notes

1. A COMMITMENT TO CHANGE

George Kennan, *Around the Cragged Hill* (New York: W. W. Norton, 1993), 259.

1. Melissa Jones, Michael Smith, and Suzanne Korosec, *2005 Integrated Energy Policy Report* (Sacramento: California Energy Commission, November 2005), 8.

2. American Lung Association, *Trends in Asthma Morbidity and Mortality* (American Lung Association, Epidemiology and Statistics Unit, Research and Program Services, July 2006), 8.

3. American Lung Association, *Trends in Asthma Morbidity and Mortality*, 8.

4. *Singapore Green Plan 2012*, http://www.mewr.gov.sg/sgp2012/index_2006.htm.

5. *Singapore Green Plan 2012*, http://www.mewr.gov.sg/sgp2012/index_2006.htm.

2. SUSTAINABILITY

1. Herman E. Daly and John B. Cobb, Jr., *For the Common Good: Redirecting the Economy toward Community, the Environment, and a Sustainable Future* (Boston Beacon Press, 1989), 71.

2. Herman E. Daly, Invited Address, World Bank, Washington DC, April 30, 2002.

3. *Worldwatch Institute's Vital Signs 2003*, 41.

4. Find Redefining Progress on the Internet at http://www.rprogress.org.

5. Worldwatch Institute, February 14, 2006, http://www.worldwatch.org/node/3881.

3. HEALTH PLUS ENVIRONMENT EQUALS SECURITY

Frank Ackerman and Lisa Heinzerling, *Priceless* (New York: The New Press, 2004), 180.

1. Jared Diamond, *Collapse* (New York: Viking Press, 2005), 79.

2. Janet Larsen, "Coal Takes a Heavy Human Toll" (Washington DC: Earth Policy Institute, August 24, 2004).

3. Environmental Protection Agency, "Controlling Power Plant Emissions Overview" (Washington DC: Environmental Protection Agency, July 5, 2006).

4. Leonardo Trasande, Philip J. Landrigan, and Clyde Schechter, "Public Health and Economic Consequences of Methyl Mercury Toxicity to the Developing Brain," *Environmental Health Perspectives* 113, no. 5, http://www.ehponline.org (May 2005).

5. *Multinational Monitor* 5, no. 9 (September 1984).

6. Henetz, Patty, "A Poison Wind, Toxic Mercury Blows into Utah from Nevada," *Salt Lake (City) Tribune*, May 1, 2005.

7. *Clean Air Initiative for Asian Cities*, http://www.cleanairnet.org/caiasia/1412/article-70771.html.

4. A GREEN PLAN PREDECESSOR

1. Joel R. Seton, *The California Energy Conservation and Renewable Energy Resource Development Program 1980–88* (San Francisco: Resource Renewal Institute, 1988), 1.

2. "Investing for Prosperity: An Update" (Sacramento: California Department of Resources, 1982), 1–16.

3. Seton, *California Energy Conservation and Renewable Energy Resource Development Program*, 31–32.

4. Professor Jeff Romm, Department of Forestry, University of California, personal conversation.

5. "Investing for Prosperity," 1–2.

6. Seton, *California Energy Conservation and Renewable Energy Resource Development Program*, 5.

7. Seton, *California Energy Conservation and Renewable Energy Resource Development Program*, preface.

8. Sin Meng Srun, *An Evaluation of the Performance of the California Forest Improvement Program* (Arcata CA: Humboldt State University, Department of Forestry, 1986), 13.

9. "Investing for Prosperity: Results 1977–1987" (San Francisco: Resource Renewal Institute, 1988).

5. THE NETHERLANDS

1. Peter Winsemius and Ulrich Guntram, *A Thousand Shades of Green: Sustainable Strategies for Competitive Advantage* (London: Earthscan Publications, May 2002).

2. *Future Environment Agenda: Clean, Clever, Competitive*, (The Hague: Ministry of VROM, 2006), http://www.vrom.nl.

3. VROM International, Netherlands Ministry of Housing, Spatial Planning, and the Environment, http://www.international .vrom.nl/pagina.html?id=10325.

4. *Statistical Yearbook of the Netherlands 2005* (Voorburg, Netherlands: Statistics Netherlands, 2005), 10.

5. *Statistical Yearbook of the Netherlands 2005*, 117.

6. Johannes Van Zijst, Counselor for Health and Environment, Royal Netherlands Embassy, personal conversation, January 2007.

7. RIVM, http://www.rivm.nl/en/.

8. VROM International, http://www.international.vrom.nl/ pagina.html?id=7542.

9. *Summary Environmental Balance 2004*, (Bilthoven: Environment Assessment Agency, National Institute for Public Health and Environment, 2004), 5.

10. Ministry of Housing, Spatial Planning, and Environment, *National Environmental Policy Plan Plus, 1990–1994* (The Hague: Ministry of Housing, Physical Planning, and Environment, 1990), 93, table 5.1.

11. *Environmental Balance 2004*, 11.

12. VROM International, http://www.sharedspaces.nl/pagina .html?id=9507.

13. *Statistical Yearbook of the Netherlands 2005.*

14. Information on Queen Beatrix's speech is from Johannes van Zijst, who also provided much of the background on the events leading up to the passage of the NEPP and on the main elements of the NEPP itself.

15. Fourth National Environmental Policy Plan (NEPP4), Summary (Bilthoven: Netherlands Ministry of Housing, Spatial Planning, and the Environment, 2001), 2.

16. World Commission on Environment and Development, *Our Common Future* (Oxford: Oxford University Press, 1987).

17. *Policy Document on Environment and Economy* (The Hague: Ministry of Housing, Spatial Planning, and the Environment, 1997).

18. Environmental Data Compendium, http://www.mnp.nl/ mnc/I-en-0360.html.

19. Ministry of Housing, Spatial Planning, and the Environment, *National Environmental Policy Plan Plus, 1990–1994.*

20. Ministry of Housing, Spatial Planning, and the Environment, *To Choose or To Lose: National Environmental Policy Plan, 1990–1994* (The Hague: SDU Publishers, 1989), 12.

21. Van Zijst, personal conversation.

22. See detailed breakdowns in *Statistical Yearbook of the Netherlands 2005,* 195.

23. *Statistical Yearbook of the Netherlands 2005,* 200.

24. *Statistical Yearbook of the Netherlands 2005,* 200.

25. See *To Choose or To Lose,* pp. 94, 96, and 97, respectively.

26. Marlise Simons, "Dutch Do the Unthinkable: Sea Is Let In," *New York Times,* March 7, 1993.

27. Ministry of Housing, Spatial Planning, and Environment, *Toward a Sustainable Netherlands: Environmental Policy Development and Implementation* (The Hague: 1994), 19 and 13, respectively.

1. Management is a key word here. To illustrate, in the debate over the legislative bill, one elderly senator said the only thing that would get his vote was a bill that would manage New Zealand resources for a better future and the act passed with his vote. An example of this result is that resource management in New Zealand is now based on districts defined by watersheds, rather than arbitrary political boundaries.

2. Information regarding New Zealand's natural history and environmental problems is taken from *Ecological Principles For Resource Management* by Karen Cronin (Wellington: Ministry for the Environment, 1988); from "National Policy and Sustainable Development: Fact or Fantasy," a paper presented by Deputy Secretary for the Environment Lindsay J. A. Gow to the State University of New York at Binghamton (1992); and from personal communications with Mr. Gow.

3. Ministry of Agriculture and Forestry, http://www.maf.govt.nz/forestry/.

4. "New Zealand Biodiversity: Executive Summary," http://www.biodiversity.govt.nz/picture/doing/nzbs/summary.html.

5. D. J. Floor Anthoni, "Timeline of Degradation Events in New Zealand," http://www.seafriends.org.nz/issues/cons/timeline.html.

6. Ministry for the Environment, *Landfills*, http://www.mfe.govt.nz/issues/waste/landfills.

7. Gow, "National Policy and Sustainable Development," 3.

8. Gow, "National Policy and Sustainable Development," 2.

9. From a personal conversation with Craig Lawson, Manager, Resource Management Directorate, New Zealand's Ministry for the Environment.

10. Information on the workings of the RMA comes from three sources: Lindsay Gow's paper "National Policy and Sustainable Development"; "New Zealand's Resource Management Act: Key Provisions and Their Implications," an address by Mr. Gow to the Australian Planning Ministers' Conference (1991); and personal communications between the author and Mr. Gow.

11. Between 2006 and 2007, the parliamentary commissioner for the environment reviewed New Zealand's progress, and the final report, "Creating Our Future: Sustainable Development for New Zealand," was released in April 2008.

12. New Zealand Ministry for the Environment, *New Zealand's Greenhouse Gas Inventory 1990–2004* (Wellington: Ministry of the Environment, April, 2006), 4.

13. Public Affairs Unit, Ministry of the Environment, http://www.cyberplace.org.nz/environment/env2010.html.

7. TOWARD A SUSTAINABLE SINGAPORE

Environment Minister Lim Swee Say, at the launch of SGP 2012, August 24, 2002.

1. Most of the information on Singapore's policies is from *The Singapore Green Plan: Toward a Model Green City* (Singapore: SNP Publishers, 1992).

2. Ministry of the Environment and Water Resources, *Singapore Green Plan 2012*, 2006 edition (Singapore: Ministry of the Environment 2006), 5.

3. Ministry of the Environment and Water Resources, *Singapore Green Plan 2012*.

4. Ministry of the Environment, *Singapore Green Plan 2012*, 15.

5. *Asian Biodiversity Special Report, Singapore: Making the Environment a Priority*, July–September 2002(Singapore: Asian Regional Centre for Biodiversity Conservation, 2002), 1, http://www.google.com/custom?q=Making+the++Environment+a+Priority.

6. Stan Sesser, "Grey Skies Ahead" (Hong Kong: Clean Air Initiative for Asian Cities, November, 2004), http://www.cleanairnet.org/caiasia/1412/article-59073.html.

7. Brian Bremmer, "China's Booming Car Market Defies Pundits" (Business Week Online, July 11, 2006).

8. *Parliamentarians for Global Action, A Singapore Case Study: Cleaning Up Air Pollution in a Generation* (Johannesburg: Parliamentarians for Global Action, August 2002), 12.

9. Ministry of the Environment, private communication.

10. Ministry of the Environment, private communication.

11. Ministry of the Environment, *Singapore Green Plan 2012*, 12.

12. Richard Seah, "The Green Side of Lee Kuan Yew" (Asian Advertising & Marketing, September 1991).

8. EUROPEAN UNION ENVIRONMENTAL POLICY

1. European Union, *Treaty of Amsterdam* (Luxembourg: Office for Official Publications of the European Communities, 1997).

2. See DEFRA, "An Operator's Guide To the EU Emissions Trading Scheme" (London: Department for Environment, Food, and Rural Affairs, February 2006).

3. See Commission Staff Working Paper, "Better Regulation and the Thematic Strategies for the Environment" (Brussels: Commission of the European Communities, September 28, 2005).

4. Http://www.europa.eu.

5. EEA countries include all European Union countries, as the EEA is an organ of the EU, and can include others. Currently, the twenty-five EU states plus Norway and Liechtenstein are EEA members.

6. "Environmental Policy Review" (Brussels: European Commission, February 2005).

7. Volker Heydt and Kristina Savikaite, *Treaty Establishing the European Community*, Article 174, ex Article 130r, of the European Commission Treaty (Brussels: The European Convention, July 2003)

8. "Mid Term Review of the European Environment and Health Action Plan 2004–2010" (Brussels: Commission of the European Communities, June 11, 2007). The conclusion notes that "the strengthened cooperation between the environment, health, and research fields at community and member states level is a true achievement."

9. Jacqueline MacGlade, executive director, European Environment Agency, "The Contribution of Policy Effectiveness Evaluation

to Better Regulation"(speech delivered in Copenhagen, October 7, 2005).

10. Stefan Lechtenbohmer, Vanessa Grimm, Dirk Mitze, Stefan Thomas, and Matthias Wissner, *Target 2020: Policies and Measures to Reduce Greenhouse Gas Emissions in the European Union* (Wuppertal: Wuppertal Institute for Climate, Environment, and Energy, September 2005), http://www.wupperinst.org.

11. Alyssa Gilvert, Jan-Wilhelm Bode, and Dian Phylipsen, *Allocation Plans for the eu Emissions Trading Scheme*, ECO FYS, Ecofys UK, http://www.ecofys.co.uk.

12. European Commission, enterprise directorate general, environment directorate general, "Why Do We Need REACH?" http://www.ecb.jrc.it/REACH, September 15, 2004.

13. "Downstream users" are companies that buy chemicals and use them as ingredients in their own products or use chemicals in an industrial or professional way.

AFTERWORD TO THE THIRD EDITION

1. See p. 131 of Jeff Goodell's *Big Coal: The Dirty Secret Behind America's Energy Future* (New York: Houghton Mifflin, 2006) in which George W. Bush's appointee, C. Boyden Gray, is reported as heading a campaign to block improved air-quality standards.

Index

abatement at the source principle, 111
accountability, in Netherlands, 125
acidification and acid rain: in California, 65; in Netherlands, 115; and security, 50, 60
acidifying gases, in EU, 169
action program committees (APCs) in Singapore, 157
Agenda 21 programs, 26, 45–46
agricultural industries: in California, 65, 73, 74; and energy policy, 19; in EU, 167; in Netherlands, 118; in New Zealand, 133, 139, 149–50; political and power concerns of, 20
agricultural runoff, in Netherlands, 92, 116
agricultural subsidies, in New Zealand, 133, 150
air pollution: in California, 65, 66; in China and India, 39, 40, 59, 160; complexity and energy policy, 19; in EU, 167, 169, 171, 174; and forests, 18; in Netherlands,

7, 92–93; over boundaries, 86–87, 106, 115–16; in Singapore, 157
air-quality standards, in Singapore, 156, 159–60
alternative energy sources, in California, 67, 72
ammonia emissions, in Netherlands, 118
Anasazi. *See* Ancient Puebloan civilization
Ancient Puebloan civilization, 50
animal waste, in Netherlands, 116. *See also* livestock farming
Apollo 8 mission pictures, 32
Arctic regions: mercury contamination in, 51; synthetic chemicals in breast milk in, 174
asbestos, in Netherlands, 117
asthma, 60
audits: in Netherlands, 88–89, 125; in Singapore, 158. *See also* monitoring of long-term targets
Audubon Society, for California IFP, 69
automobile emissions: and

automobile emissions (*cont.*)
disease, 60; in EU, 170; in
Netherlands, 92–93, 97, 105,
115; in Singapore, 159–60
automobiles, disposal of, in
Netherlands, 110, 127

"backcasting" in NEPP, 110
balance of powers, 10–12; in
EU, 164, 171–73; failure of,
in Canada, 31; in Singapore,
159
Bank of America, 180
beach erosion control, in California, 73
Beatrix, Queen of Netherlands,
6, 94–95, 96
best practicable means principle, 111
biodiversity: in EU, 169; in
Netherlands, 94; in New
Zealand, 134–35, 149, 153;
in Singapore, 158–59
biomass energy sources, and
California IFP, 67, 72
bird flu, 60–61
Brandt, Willy, 33
Brown, Edmund G. (Jerry), 63
Brundtland Report: definition
of sustainable development
in, 32; and energy shortage,
57; and growth, 34; and
Netherlands, 84, 100–101;
as philosophical statement,
not action plan, 41

building trades as NEPP target
group, 118
Bush (George W.) administration, 167–68
business groups. *See* trade and
employer associations
business sector. *See* industrial
and business sector

California: automobile pollution and asthma in, 60;
background, 64–65; energy
policy of, 18–19, 67–68;
lack of comprehensive ap-
proach in, 22–23
California Investing for Prosperity (IFP) program, 66–75;
overview of legislation,
71–74; passage of legislation, 68–70
California Office for Appropriate Technology, 67
California Resources Agency:
background, 63–64, 74;
programs, 66–68
California State Energy Commission, 67
campaign contributions, 56
Canada: failure of plan in, xii,
31; funding commitment
in, 25–26; funding of nongovernmental organizations
in, 124
carbon-dioxide emissions: in
EU, 172–73; in Netherlands,

91, 127, 128; in New Zealand, 149. *See also* greenhouse gas emissions

carbon-dioxide emissions trading, 86; in EU, 166, 173–74

carbon-dioxide tax, in Netherlands, 104, 128

carrying capacity of land, 50–51

chambers of commerce. *See* trade and employer associations

change: effect of, on U.S., 13–14; as key to survival, 9

chemical pollution policy in EU, 165, 170, 174–77

Chernoble, accident at, 57

China: air pollution in, 59, 160; industrial development in, 39–40; mercury pollution in, 53; and population growth, 47

chlorfluorocarbons. *See* greenhouse gas emissions

civic groups, in Singapore, 158. *See also* public organizations

"Clean, Clever, Competitive" approach, in Netherlands, 85, 172

climate change: and EU, 165, 169, 170, 173; in NEPP, 115; in New Zealand, 148, 149, 153; in Singapore, 157

CNG (compressed natural gas), in Singapore, 160

coal-burning energy plants: and mercury contamination, 51, 53, 56; in Netherlands, 115. *See also* fossil fuel industries

coastal resources, and California IFP, 72

cogeneration projects: and California IFP, 67, 72; in Netherlands, 110

complexity, addressing, xiv, 17–18, 20–21

comprehensive plans, 17–21; importance of, xiii, 8–9; in Netherlands, 100, 107–9, 126–28; in New Zealand, 140–44

compressed natural gas (CNG), in Singapore, 160

Concern for Tomorrow report (Netherlands), 95–96, 114

Conference on the Human Environment (Stockholm, 1972), 34

consensus building: in Netherlands, 88, 97–99; in New Zealand, 136–37

constituencies, building of, for California IFP, 69–70

consumers, in Netherlands, 118, 122–23

consumption: of energy in California, 64; reduction of, 44; and shortages/security, 59–60

continental scale in NEPP, 114,
115–16
cooperation among interests,
11–12; in Netherlands, 44,
88, 104–5, 121–22, 127–28
cost-effectiveness of policy, in
EU, 173–74
"customized implementation,"
114

Daly, Herman, 35–36
DDT, in Netherlands, 92
decoupling economic growth
from bad effects, in Netherlands, 89, 91–92
deforestation: and acid rain,
60; in EU, 168; and Singapore, 162. See also forest
industry
dehydration, 115
deregulation, 5
desalinization, in Singapore,
160
developed countries: need to
set example, 40–41; and
population growth, 47
developing countries: and
equitable distribution of
wealth, 33, 36; and population growth, 46–48; and
resource use, 34, 153–54;
and security, 58; and UN
Development Programme,
46; unsustainable practices
in, 39–41

development and environment.
See sustainable development
diesel fuels, in Netherlands, 93
dioxins, in Netherlands, 92
diseases: epidemics, 60–61; and
security threats, 50–51. See
also health concerns
drift nets, 72–73

Easter Island, 50
ecological footprints, 37–39
economic concerns: considered
within environmental con-
cerns, 35; in EU, 173–74; in
Netherlands, 85; success of
green planning, 39–41
economic cooperation and
political cooperation, in EU,
165
economic growth: in California, 22; and human well-being, 35–36; in NEPP, 89, 104
economic policy and envi-
ronmental policy, xii; in
Netherlands, 85; in New
Zealand, 152
EEA (European Environment
Agency), 169, 172–73
effect-oriented measures, 113
Ehrlich, Paul and Anne, 33
emergency information and
help network, in EU, 170
emissions reduction: in Netherlands, 44, 82, 84, 89,
91–92, 96, 104–5, 118; in

European Union (EU), 163–77; approach to environment, 169–70; background, 164–65; and carbon-dioxide emissions, 128; and deforestation, 60; as example for U.S., 165–66; and influence of Netherlands, 86; and influence on U.S. industry, 13; and peace issues, 37; and planning, 38–39; and relation of economy and environment, 85; and thematic strategies, 171

eutrophication, in Netherlands, 93, 115, 116, 117

farming. *See* agricultural industries

farm machinery use, in New Zealand, 133

Federated Farmers (New Zealand), 139

feedback mechanisms, 44

fertilizer use: in Netherlands, 116; in New Zealand, 133, 139, 150

fisheries: in California, 64, 72–73; and comprehensiveness, 18; in EU, 167; and global warming, 5; mercury contamination, 53–55; in Netherlands, 91; in New Zealand, 135, 153. *See also* salmon fisheries

flexibility: advantages of,

8–9; and implementation of plans, 21; in Netherlands, 98, 107, 113

flooding: in EU, 168; in New Zealand, 134, 141;

fluvial (watershed) scale, in Netherlands, 114, 116, 117

forest industry: in California, 65, 66, 69–70, 71, 72, 73; and comprehensiveness, 18; and energy policy, 19; in EU, 167; in Netherlands, 126; in New Zealand, 134, 149–50, 152. *See also* deforestation

formaldehyde, 117

fossil fuel industries: and coal-burning energy plants, 51, 53, 56; and economy *vs.* environment/economic concerns, 35; and EU, 167; and global warming, 9–10; in Netherlands, 115; and shortages, 59; and short-term outlook, 5; in U.S., 13. *See also* oil industry

Four Taps Strategy, 160

France, iron and coal shortages in, 37

funding commitments, 25–26

future of the world: and sustainability, 46–48

General Electric, 180

General Motors, 10

generations, solidarity between, in Netherlands, 44, 84, 99, 101

geographic scale in planning, 114–18

geothermal energy sources, in California, 67, 71, 72

Germany: forests in, 18; iron and coal shortages in, 37; solar energy in, 179–80

global emission reductions: and EU, 173

global scale in planning: in Netherlands, 114; and Singapore, 157. See also international cooperation; transboundary pollution

global warming: and EU, 170; as global problem, 4–5; and Netherlands, 7, 87, 115

goals: importance of, 22; in Netherlands, 83, 98, 112; in New Zealand, 142, 144, 153

government: and balance of powers, 11–12; large-scale commitment by, xiii–xiv, 23–26

government agencies, and California IFP, 74–75

government employees, in Netherlands, 98–99

government leadership, 24–26; and California IFP, 75; fail-

ure to act by, 5; in Netherlands, 6, 96

greenhouse effect, 115

greenhouse gas emissions: in Netherlands, 108; in EU, 169

Green Plans: approaches to, 41–45; basic elements of, 16–24, 26; definition of, 14, 82; importance of, xii–xiii; as model of success, 15

"green taxes" in Netherlands, 104, 128

growth. See economic growth; limits to growth; population growth; sustainable growth

growth hormones in beef, and EU, 168

hazardous substances: and EU, 171, 176; in New Zealand, 148. See also toxic substance pollution

health concerns, 49–62; and energy policy, 19; as environmental problem, 31; and epidemics, 60–61; in EU, 168, 170, 171, 174–75; and mercury toxicity, 52–53; in Netherlands, 86, 106; in New Zealand, 153; and public education, 55–56; and security, 50–56; in Singapore, 157, 161

Hewlett Packard, 13, 180

history, learning from, 56–57
hormones in beef exports, and
EU, 176
hydrochlorfluorcarbons. *See*
greenhouse gas emissions

IFP. *See* California Investing for
Prosperity (IFP) program
India: air pollution in, 59, 160;
industrial development in,
39
indoor environmental pollutants, 117
industrial accidents, in EU, 170
industrial and business sector:
and California IFP, 67–68,
69; as crucial to success of
environmental recovery,
9–10; Green companies
in, 180; and opposition to
environmental problems, 5;
in Singapore, 156; in U.S.,
non-leadership by, 120
industrialization: disadvan-
tages, 4–5
industrialized countries: and
equitable distribution of
wealth, 36–38, 142
industrial sector in Netherlands: and cooperation with
other interests, 88; and
environmental watchdogs,
12; leadership by, 119–20;
and long-term perspective,
84–85, 119; and negotia-

tion of environmental goals,
121–22; stability and flexibility for, 82–83; and support for plan, 6, 86, 96–97;
as target group, 118
information-management systems, in Singapore, 161
integrated lifecycle management, in Netherlands, 44,
109–10, 127
integrated pest management, in
California, 73
integration of efforts, xii, 21–
24; in EU, 171; importance
of, xiii; in Netherlands, 100,
101–3; in New Zealand,
141; in Singapore, 158
internalization of environmental concerns principle, 111,
113–14
international cooperation:
Agenda 21 programs,
45–46; and airborne toxins,
115–16; and Netherlands,
151; and New Zealand,
151; and Singapore, 157.
See also global scale in planning; transboundary pol-
lution
Investing for Prosperity. *See*
California Investing for
Prosperity (IFP) program
irrigation, in New Zealand,
133, 150

Japan: disease outbreaks, 61; mercury contamination, 51, 54–55, 56

Kyoto Protocol: and EU, 13, 85, 169, 173; in New Zealand, 149

labor unions: and California IFP, 69, 73; in Netherlands, 6, 88, 124; in Singapore, 158
land resources, in New Zealand, 153
land-use policies, in Singapore, 156, 159. *See also* zoning laws
large-scale commitment by government, xiii–xiv, 23–26
leadership, xii. *See also* government leadership
League of Women Voters, 69
Lee Kuan Yew, 162
legislative process, and big-picture approach, 7–8
Leopold, Aldo, 32
level playing field, xii. *See also* equitable distribution of wealth
lifecycle management approach, in Netherlands, 44, 109–10, 127
limits to growth: and environmental movement, 33; and Herman Daly, 35–36; *vs.* sustainability, 30–31

Limits to Growth (MIT), 33
livestock farming: and beef exports to EU, 176; in Netherlands, 87, 116; in New Zealand, 133; in U.S., 168
lobbyists, 7
local government, 23–24
local scale, 114
long-term targets: advantages of, xii, 6–7; in Netherlands, 84–85, 108–9, 119
Lubbers (Rudd) government (Netherlands), 95

Maathai, Wangari, 36–37
Mad Cow Disease (bovine spongiform encephalopathy), 50
malaria, 60
Maori, 132, 137–38
marine environments, in EU, 171
market dynamism in NEPP3, 104–5
Marsh, George Perkins, 32
mass migrations, 46–47
Mayan civilization, 50
mercury contamination, 51–55
metal industry, in Netherlands, 119
methane. *See* greenhouse gas emissions
Minimata, Japan, 51, 54–55
mining activities, in New Zealand, 148–49

Ministry of Public Works and
Water Management (Neth-
erlands), 92
Minnesota, 164
monitoring of long-term targets: in Netherlands, 88–89,
108–9, 124–26; in New
Zealand, 146–48; in Singapore, 159–60
Muir, John, 32

National Allocations Plans in
EU, 174
National Coastal Policy State-
ment (New Zealand), 151
National Development Act
(New Zealand), 130
National Ecological Network
(NEN) in Netherlands, 94
National Energy Efficiency
Committee (Singapore), 160
National Environmental Policy
Plan. See NEPP (National
Environmental Policy Plan)
(1989–90) (Netherlands)
National Spatial Strategy and
Agenda for a Living Coun-
tryside Policy (Netherlands),
94
native plants: in New Zealand,
134–35; in Singapore, 158
natural resources, EU thematic
strategy, 170, 171
Nature Conservancy, 10–11,
12

nature conservation: in EU,
170; in Singapore, 157,
158–59. See also wildlife
and wildlife habitat
NEN (National Ecological Network) in Netherlands, 94
NEPP (National Environmental Policy Plan) (1989–90)
(Netherlands): as example,
xi–xii; and integration, 101–
3; monitoring of, 85–89;
philosophical basis for, 100,
108; political basis of, 94–
96; principles of, 111–12;
as response to Brundtland
Report, 43–45; structure of,
109–11; support for, 96–97;
and target-group approach,
118–21; "themes," targets,
and goals for, 114, 117; "To
Choose or to Lose" slogan,
99, 119; and updates, 103–
6, 124–26
NEPP+ (1990), 103–4, 114
NEPP3 (1998), 104–5
NEPP4 (2001) "Where There's
a Will, There's a World,"
89–91, 98, 99, 105–6, 111
Netherlands, 79–128; com-
prehensiveness in, 20, 21;
cooperation among interests
in, 11–12; as example, 6,
14, 15, 16, 38; government
commitment in, 25; indus-
trial sector in, 9–10, 12;

influence of Brundtland Report in, 100–101; political courage in, 136; remaining problems in, 89–91; Rhine River cleanup in, 24; technical approach to, 41, 43–45. *See also* NEPP (National Environmental Policy Plan) (1989–90) (Netherlands)

New Jersey, 164

New Zealand, 129–54; and Agenda 21 programs, 46; comprehensiveness in, 21; environmental problems in, 132–35; as example, 14, 15, 16, 38; government, 137, 141–42, 145; political courage in, 136; and programs outside of RMA, 148–49; and progress toward sustainability, 149–50; public hearings in, 68; resource dependence in, 132, 133; structural approach to planning in, 41, 42–43, 130. *See also* Resource Management Act (RMA) (New Zealand)

New Zealand 2010 program, 152–54

New Zealand Coastal Policy Statement, 144

nitrogen deposits from agriculture, in Netherlands, 116

nitrogen dioxide, in Netherlands, 92

nitrous oxide, in EU, 169. *See also* greenhouse gas emissions

noise reduction: in EU, 170; in Netherlands, 92, 115, 117

nongovernmental organizations: in Netherlands, 124; in Singapore, 157–58. *See also* nonprofit environmental groups

nonprofit environmental groups: in Netherlands, 6; in New Zealand, 140. *See also* environmental groups

North-South (Brandt), 33

nuclear accidents, 57, 118

nuclear waste: and California IFP, 64–65; in Netherlands, 115

Nuisance Act (Netherlands), 101–2, 115

odor reduction, in Netherlands, 101–2, 115, 117

OECD (Organisation for Economic Co-operation and Development), 47

oil embargo of 1970s, 64

oil industry, 20. *See also* fossil fuel industries

oil resources and security, 59

options, keeping open, in Netherlands, 105–6

Oregon, 164

lands, 87, 93, 117; in New Zealand, 143; in Singapore, 162

population growth, 46–48; and carrying capacity of land, 51; in Singapore, 159

Population Resources, Environments (Ehrlich and Ehrlich), 33

post-Kyoto goals in EU, 172

prevention of pollution problems principle, 4–5; in Netherlands, 108, 111

principle of portions, 72

printing industry, in Netherlands, 119

priorities, setting, in Netherlands, 114

privately owned property, in New Zealand, 143

privatization, 24

product lifecycle analysis, 34

product quality, in Netherlands, 110

public cooperation and support, xiii; and California IFP program, 67–68; in Netherlands, 96, 97, 99, 104–5, 131; in New Zealand, 131, 154; in Singapore, 157

public demand for action, 55–56

public education: in EU, 170; on health threats, 55–56; in Netherlands, 123–24; in

New Zealand, 140; in Singapore, 156

public health. *See* health concerns

public hearings, in New Zealand, 68, 136

public internalization of environmental concerns, 111

public opinion, in Netherlands, 7, 83

public organizations, in Netherlands, 118. *See also* civic groups

quality of life, in Singapore, 161

quality promotion, 44

radiation, in EU, 171

rapid transit. *See* transit system policies

REACH (Registration, Evaluation, Authorization, and Restriction of Chemicals) program, 174–75

real-estate development, in New Zealand, 139

recreation. *See* parks and recreation

recycling and reuse: in Netherlands, 20, 109–10, 117; in Singapore, 160–61

Redefining Progress, 37–39

regional government: in Netherlands, 94, 106; in New

Severe Acute Respiratory Syndrome (SARS), 50
sewerage: in Netherlands, 115; in Singapore, 160
SGP2012 (Singapore Green Plan), 155–62
sheep, in New Zealand, 133
shortages of resources: in history, 37; and security, 56–61
short-term targets, xii
Silicon Valley manufacturers and EU, 13, 176
Singapore: comprehensiveness in, 21; as example, 14, 15, 16, 38; funding commitment, 25; political courage in, 136
Singapore Green Plan (SGP2012), 155–62
single-issue concerns, 17
Small Is Beautiful (Schumacher), 33
social change, in Netherlands, 112–14
social contract, in Netherlands, 81
social inequities, in New Zealand, 142
soil clean-up: in EU, 168, 174; in Netherlands, 108, 115, 117, 126–27
soil conservation: and California IFP, 72, 73; and government commitment, 25
soil erosion, in EU, 168
soil policies, in California, 22

soil problems, in New Zealand, 134
soil protection: in EU, 171; political and power concerns of, 20
soil salinity, in California, 66
solar energy: and California IFP, 67, 72; in Germany, 179–80
solid-waste management, in Netherlands, 20, 91, 108, 115, 117
source-oriented measures, 111, 113
speed limits, in Netherlands, 92–93
squandering of resources, 115
stakeholders, participation by, xii; in Netherlands, 81, 85, 102; in Singapore, 157
standards for performance: advantages of, 6–7; in EU, 166; in New Zealand, 143, 144–45, 151
stand-still principle, 111
steelhead restoration projects, in California, 72
stewardship of resources: and California IFP, 64, 70; in Netherlands, 123
Sudan, 37, 51, 60
sulfur dioxide, in EU, 169
sustainability, 27–48; and United States, 179
sustainability indicators, 44

"Sustainable Action Progress
Report, 2005" (Nether-
lands), 45
sustainable development: definition of, 29–32; in EU, 164;
as goal in New Zealand,
142–43; Herman Daly on,
35–36; history of concept
of, 32–34; in Netherlands,
101; as solution, 38–39
sustainable growth, in EU, 170
sustainable management
(Brundtland Report), 57
sustainable management in
New Zealand, 42, 129,
141, 187n1; definition of,
142–43
systems thinking, 17

target-group approach, in
Netherlands, 114, 118–22,
127
taxation system, in Netherlands, 104, 128
taxpayer rebellion, and California IFP program, 68, 74
technology applications: in EU,
165; in Netherlands, 114,
121–22; in New Zealand,
141
TEU (Treaty of the European
Union), 170
thematic strategies, in EU, 165,
167, 171
themes (environmental prob-

lem areas), in Netherlands,
44, 114–15. See also *specific
themes* (e.g. acidification
and acid rain)
Thoreau, Henry David, 32
tidelands oil revenues: and
California IFP, 71
time-bound long-term targets,
in Netherlands, 81
time horizon, long, 7
tobacco industry, 54
tobacco smoke, 117
toxic substance pollution: in
EU, 171; in Netherlands, 92,
100, 115; transboundary
scale of, 116–17. See also
hazardous substances
trade and employer associations: in Netherlands, 119,
124; in New Zealand,
138–39
traffic and transport, in Netherlands, 92, 95, 118
transboundary pollution: and
Netherlands, 86–87, 106,
115–16. See also global
scale in planning; international cooperation
"transition" management in
Netherlands, 105–6
transit system policies: in
California, 22; in Singapore,
156
Treaty of the European Union
(TEU), 170

two-track principle, 111, 113

UN Development Programme, and developing countries, 46
UN Earth Summit in Rio (1992), 26, 34; and sustainable development discussions, 45–46
UN Economic Commission for Europe, and transboundary pollution, 116
UN Environmental Programme, 34
Unilever, 83
Union Carbide, 12
United States: economic boom *vs.* cost of lifestyle in, 38; effect of EU policies on, 168, 176; and environmental problems in Asia, 40; EU as example for, 165–66; of failure to sign UN Earth Summit in Rio (1992), 34; and fossil fuel industries, 13; government commitment in, 25; and implications of Green Plans, 179; lack of federal environmental policy in, 164, 176–77; lack of progress in, xii; and long-term thinking, 9–10; mercury poisoning in, 52, 53–54, 55–56; and monitoring of results, 88–89; priorities of environmental movement

in, 124; real-estate development in, 139; relation of government to industry in, 120–21; and single-issue approach to environment, 100, 167
UN World Commission on Environment and Development, 29; influence on Netherlands of, 100–101
urban environment, in EU thematic strategy, 170, 171
urban resources: and California IFP, 73, 74; in Netherlands, 93; in Singapore, 159
U.S. Chamber of Commerce, 120–21, 168
Utah, mercury poisoning, 55, 56

Volkswagen, 110, 127

war and peace, 36–37
waste management: in EU thematic strategy, 170, 171; in Netherlands, 100, 111, 113, 115; in New Zealand, 135, 148; in Singapore, 157, 160–61
watchdog function: and balance of powers, 12; in Netherlands, 89; in New Zealand, 140; in Singapore, 157–58; in U.S., 88. *See also* environmental groups; nonprofit environmental groups

Economic Thresholds for Integrated Pest Management
Edited by Leon G. Higley and Larry P. Pedigo

Ecology and Economics of the Great Plains
Daniel S. Licht

Uphill against Water: The Great Dakota Water War
Peter Carrels

Changing the Way America Farms: Knowledge and Community in the Sustainable Agriculture Movement
Neva Hassanein

Ogallala: Water for a Dry Land, second edition
John Opie

Willard Cochrane and the American Family Farm
Richard A. Levins

Down and Out on the Family Farm: Rural Rehabilitation in the Great Plains, 1929–1945
Michael Johnston Grant

Raising a Stink: The Struggle over Factory Hog Farms in Nebraska
Carolyn Johnsen

The Curse of American Agricultural Abundance: A Sustainable Solution
Willard W. Cochrane

Good Growing: Why Organic Farming Works
Leslie A. Duram

Roots of Change: Nebraska's New Agriculture
  Mary Ridder

Remaking American Communities: A Reference Guide to Urban Sprawl
  Edited by David C. Soule
  Foreword by Neal Peirce

Remaking the North American Food System: Strategies for Sustainability
  Edited by C. Clare Hinrichs and Thomas A. Lyson

Crisis and Opportunity: Sustainability in American Agriculture
  John E. Ikerd

Green Plans: Blueprint for a Sustainable Earth, revised and updated
  Huey D. Johnson
  With a new afterword by the author